MW00466211

I love Luke's writing of the gospel account because he was consistently giving us a glimpse into the prayer life of Jesus. He would tell of how the disciples would wake up in the morning and Jesus would be gone in a solitary place, having met with the Father all night in prayer. Inside of every believer is the same desire to be with the Father and hear His voice. It is there where we find a love that is better than life, a peace that surpasses understanding, and an overflowing joy. It's as we separate unto God and hear His voice that we discover again what we were created for. *Evenings With the Holy Spirit* by Jennifer LeClaire is a simple yet powerful resource for those desiring to do as Jesus did and step away from the daily bustle of life to spend time with the Father. Jennifer invites us on a journey that, if embraced, will refresh your soul as you draw close to the Holy Spirit and encounter the still, small voice of God in your life.

—BANNING LIEBSCHER
FOUNDER AND PASTOR, JESUS CULTURE

The Holy Spirit is to us like Jesus was to the first apostles. This devotional will jump start your intimacy with Him!

—SID ROTH
HOST, *IT'S SUPERNATURAL!*

For those of us who fancy ourselves Word-centered or theologically minded, here is a book that has much to teach us regarding the ways of the Holy Spirit. Surprise after surprise comes to those who pursue this helpful book.

—R. T. KENDALL

Some Christians are satisfied with an occasional encounter with the Holy Spirit. But this special book will help you to experience the Spirit's presence on a daily basis. The Father invites us to drink from the Spirit's flowing river every day! I pray you will be saturated with His love and power as you read *Evenings With the Holy Spirit*.

—J. Lee Grady
Former Editor, *Charisma* Magazine
Director, The Mordecai Project
Author, *Set My Heart on Fire*

Intimacy with God is vital in the hour in which we live. We need to cultivate a more accurate prophetic spirit that is sensitive to His heart so we can discern His leadership in our lives. In *Evenings With the Holy Spirit*, Jennifer LeClaire has offered us more insight into how the Holy Spirit speaks to our hearts for edification, exhortation, comfort—and at times gentle correction for the journey. These daily devotions will stir a hunger in your heart for more and inspire you to develop a deeper relationship with the Holy Spirit.

—Ryan LeStrange
Founder, Impact International
President, New Breed Revival Network
Cofounder, AwakeningTV.com

EVENINGS

WITH THE

*Holy
Spirit*

JENNIFER LeCLAIRE

CHARISMA
HOUSE

Most Charisma House Book Group products are available at special quantity discounts for bulk purchase for sales promotions, premiums, fund-raising, and educational needs. For details, write Charisma House Book Group, 600 Rinehart Road, Lake Mary, Florida 32746, or telephone (407) 333-0600.

Evenings With the Holy Spirit
 by Jennifer LeClaire
Published by Charisma House
Charisma Media/Charisma House Book Group
600 Rinehart Road
Lake Mary, Florida 32746
www.charismahouse.com

.zondervan.com The "NIV" and "New International Version" are trademarks registered in the United States Patent and Trademark Office by Biblica, Inc.™

Scripture quotations marked NKJV are taken from the New King James Version®. Copyright © 1982 by Thomas Nelson. Used by permission. All rights reserved.

Scripture quotations marked NLT are from the Holy Bible, New Living Translation, copyright © 1996, 2004, 2007. Used by permission of Tyndale House Publishers, Inc., Wheaton, IL 60189. All rights reserved.

Cover design by Lisa Rae McClure
Design Director: Justin Evans

Visit the author's website at www.jenniferleclaire.org.

Library of Congress Cataloging-in-Publication Data:
An application to register this book for cataloging has been submitted to the Library of Congress.
International Standard Book Number: 978-1-62998-965-5
E-book ISBN: 978-1-62998-966-2

First edition

16 17 18 19 20 — 987654321
Printed in China

*I dedicate this book to my daughter, Bridgette. She is the love of my life and has inspired my heart to press into the kingdom and see God's will done in our lives. She demonstrates the generous heart of the Father, the joy of the Lord, and an enduring spirit that refuses to give up. I am so blessed to call her daughter and friend.*

*W*HILE READING *Evenings With the Holy Spirit*, I found myself truly enjoying the daily opportunity to "come away" with the Holy Spirit and hear Him speak. Each evening there is a fresh word from the Lord, reminding us of our privilege and need to lean back into His presence and listen. The Scripture readings that back up the word for the evening serve also as a delightful discipline for those with a busy life to pause and meditate on the beauty and power of the Word of God.

As the church is being awakened, more and more I sense the Holy Spirit urging us to train and equip believers to anchor themselves in His Word. Too many read only familiar and favorite passages and miss out on the fullness of what the Lord has to say. The daily readings in this devotional help make sure the reader is having a varied scriptural diet. Taking these words and processing them is an important aspect of our daily walk with the Lord.

Recently I have felt the Lord reminding me to not despise prophecy (1 Thess. 5:20). We can do that so easily without realizing what we are doing.

In an age of so much information and revelation, we can fail to actually allow the Word of God to penetrate past our heads and into our hearts.

Jennifer has provided a beautiful platform here for people to hear the word of the Lord, and my encouragement would be for you to meditate on the readings for a few minutes and allow the words to sink deep into your heart. Think about how the word for the evening can be applied in your life. In doing this, we are stewarding well what the Lord is giving.

Taking a little time to chew over what we have read before rushing on to the next thought or distraction is a discipline that will allow the Word to not just be knowledge that puffs up, but revelation that becomes part of our identity. As we digest it, it becomes part of us, and as we do that, more revelation will come. As the Scripture says, to him who has, more will be given!

It is my prayer that you will enjoy your evenings with the Holy Spirit. I know that He will most certainly enjoy His time with you.

—Katherine Ruonala
Senior Leader, Glory City Church
Author, *Living in the Miraculous*, *From Wilderness to Wonders*, and *Life With the Holy Spirit*

# INTRODUCTION

$\mathcal{W}$RITING MORNINGS WITH the Holy Spirit—and engaging in 6:00 a.m. prayer calls five days a week with hundreds of people around the country and even around the world—changed my life. Each morning as I read the day's devotion, the Holy Spirit was faithful to breathe new life into the words He spoke to my heart so long ago—in some cases many, many years ago.

I was flooded with messages from people—and met many of them while traveling in itinerant ministry—who told me the Spirit-inspired words on the pages of *Mornings With the Holy Spirit* changed their lives too. During the morning prayer calls, bodies were healed, souls were delivered, enemies were defeated, and faith was stirred. Although that book is dear to my own heart, I could never have imagined the rippling impact it would have on other people, men and women alike. I always tell people it's the best book I've ever written because I didn't really write it. I merely chronicled what I heard the Holy Spirit speak to my heart.

I've kept journaling what the Holy Spirit has

spoken to me during the last two years since *Mornings With the Holy Spirit* was published, and the result is in your hands now. I've been on quite a journey for those two years—and the Holy Spirit has been faithful to speak into every circumstance of my life and encourage my heart.

Like you, I've walked through sickness—even severe sickness. I remember when doctors thought I had a serious disease and sent me for a brain MRI. I still remember lying in the scanner tube with the plastic mask over my face and thinking about how many other people had been in that same position, fighting for their lives. I still remember praising God in faith, knowing by the peace of God in my spirit that I would live and not die.

Like you, I've walked through betrayals in relationships. I've taken financial hits at inconvenient times. I've watched people I love suffer. I've faced enemy onslaughts against my mind. I've been misunderstood and persecuted. I've felt like quitting more times than I'm willing to admit. But I've also gained a greater revelation of the faithfulness of God, the love of God, the provision of God, the healing power of God, and God's unchanging character. I wouldn't trade any of those trying experiences for the experience of receiving the Father's life-changing revelations.

Since I compiled *Mornings With the Holy Spirit*, everything has changed. My prayer life has soared higher. My intimacy with the Lord has grown deeper. My sensitivity to His voice has waxed sharper. My love for the Word, my hunger to host His presence, my boldness in battle, my love for the brethren, my compassion for the lost—everything has changed. Indeed, the experience of collecting my journal entries into one book, matching them with scriptures and prayer-starters, and gathering with people morning after morning to pray through what the Spirit said and what the Word says has transformed me and many others.

God has brought me a mighty long way since I got saved in a jail cell after being falsely accused of a crime shortly after my husband abandoned me with a two-year-old baby in 1999. My attorney told me the prosecutor was recommending five years in prison, which would have made my daughter an orphan until second grade. I had hit rock bottom and decided to cry out to the same Lord I had earlier blamed for my downward spiral. See, I never really knew Him beyond His picture in my great-grandmother's living room.

While I was in the jail's general population, a team of traveling evangelists rolled through. People testified of the Lord's saving grace from heroin addiction, prostitution, and other lifestyles far worse than anything I'd lived through. I figured if He could turn their lives around, He could do the same for me. With the conviction of the Holy Spirit at work, I surrendered my life to Christ and began devouring the Word of God. Soon I would hear that still, small voice that's so familiar now tell me I would be delivered from this false imprisonment on the fortieth day. And it was just as He told me it would be. I was fully vindicated from the false charges, and the case was ruled a gross injustice. Hallelujah!

The same Holy Spirit who led me to Christ and assured my heart amid the worst trial of my life still speaks to me today. He gives me wisdom for everyday living, peace in my heart during the hard times, joy unspeakable and full of glory, revelation about the living Word of God, comfort when I am hurting, and so much more. I have come to lean and depend on Him in ways I can't fully explain. I know He is on my side—and He is on your side too.

Whatever you've been through, whatever you're going through right now, and whatever you will face in the future, you can know that you know that you know the Holy Spirit will never leave you or forsake you. He is speaking more than you know—and you can hear His voice just as I can. Jesus said, "My sheep hear My voice" (John 10:27). My prayer is that, as you read these daily entries, you will discover that the Holy Spirit wants to be part of every area of your life—and He will speak into any part of your life where you welcome Him.

Although Jesus is fully God, He did not launch His public ministry until He was baptized with the Holy Spirit. How much more, then, do we need the Holy Spirit in our lives and ministries?

> Then Jesus came from Galilee to John at the Jordan to be baptized by him. But John prohibited Him, saying, "I need to be baptized by You, and do You come to me?" But Jesus answered him, "Let it be so now, for it is fitting for us to fulfill all righteousness." Then he permitted Him. And when Jesus was baptized, He came up immediately out of the water. And suddenly the heavens were opened to Him, and He saw the Spirit of God descending on Him like a dove.
> —MATTHEW 3:13–16

The Bible says the Spirit of God, which is the Holy Spirit, descended on Him like a "dove." There you see one of the names of the Holy Spirit and one of the symbols of the Holy Spirit. But the Bible also says in the New International Version that the Spirit was "alighting on Him" (v. 16). What does that mean? It may be easier to understand this verse in the New Living Translation, where it says the Spirit of God was "settling on Him" (v. 16). The Spirit of God filled Jesus and rested upon Him. What a mighty experience! You can have that same experience.

Jesus is the baptizer, and He baptizes us with the Holy Spirit when we ask and believe. If you would like the Holy Spirit to fill you with His presence and power, pray this prayer:

*Father, I surrender full control of my life to You. I ask You even now to fill me to overflowing with Your Spirit, just as You have promised to do if I ask according to Your will. I ask this in the name of Jesus and believe that You are pouring out Your Spirit upon me right now.*

The Holy Spirit wants to help you. Before He was crucified, Jesus said He would send another Comforter (John 16:7, KJV). The Holy Spirit is described in many ways in the Bible—from breath of the Almighty (Job 33:4) to eternal Spirit (Heb. 9:14) to Spirit of grace (Zech. 12:10, NIV; Heb. 10:29). The Holy Spirit proceeds from the Father (John 15:26), which is why sometimes He is called the Spirit of God. He transforms us from glory to glory (2 Cor. 3:18). He draws us to Jesus (John 6:44). He reveals truth (Matt. 11:25). He leads and guides us (John 12:49–50). He imparts the life of Christ (John 3:5). He does all this and so much more—and, again, He wants to speak with you. He wants to fellowship with you. He wants to walk with you everywhere you go.

Like *Mornings With the Holy Spirit*, this new daily devotional contains prophetic words the Holy Spirit spoke to my heart day by day as I walked with Him. These words have encouraged me when I felt like I couldn't take another step and empowered me to take authority over enemies of my faith. These words have inspired my heart with a deeper understanding of the love, mercy, and grace of God.

My prayer is that you too will find inspiration, comfort, revelation, wisdom, and whatever else you need as you travel down the narrow road that leads to life. I pray that the Holy Spirit will make His voice loud and clear in your heart, sharpen your discernment to recognize the difference between His truth and the enemy's lies, stir your faith to totally surrender to His will, and more. Read this devotional with a pen in your hand and a "yes" in your heart. I believe He will speak what you need to hear in the moment. I believe you'll discover a new dimension of His presence and new ways He is speaking to you day in and day out.

—JENNIFER LeCLAIRE

# January

See, I will do a new thing, now it shall spring forth;
shall you not be aware of it? I will even make a
way in the wilderness, and rivers in the desert.

—Isaiah 43:19

## You Can Have Another
## New Beginning

*Y*OU CAN HAVE a new beginning. It doesn't matter how many new beginnings you've had before. Don't believe the lie that you can't have any more. Jesus's work on the cross paved the way for another new beginning and another and another—as many as you need. Our Father's mercies are new every day. Seasons change. Believe that you can have a new beginning in any area of your life that has not aligned with Father's perfect will for you. Embrace this precious promise, get back up again, and walk toward the new beginning. Father has good plans for you. It's up to you to move into His grace.

REVELATION 21:5; EPHESIANS 4:22–24;
LAMENTATIONS 3:22–23

### → PRAYER ←

*I believe I can have a new beginning because the Word of God tells me so. Help me walk in this promise as I transition from one season to another. Give me the strength to hold fast to this great and precious promise when I can't see what door to walk through. Walk with me.*

## January 2

### DELIGHT YOURSELF IN THE LORD

FATHER ALWAYS HAS something bigger and better in mind if you'll walk toward what He loves, even if that means walking away from what you think you love. Here's a promise: you'll discover that you love what He loves far more than you loved what you walked away from.

Father gives you the desires of your heart as you delight yourself in Him—and sometimes that means He changes the desires of your heart to line up with His. So delight yourself in Him because He delights Himself in you. And be willing to let go of the *good* thing for the *best* things He has planned for you.

PSALM 37:4; PSALM 20:4; EZEKIEL 36:26–27

### → PRAYER ←

*I set my heart to delight in You. Change my heart's desires to match Your heart's desires. Give me the desires of Your heart so that You can give me the desires of my heart. I surrender to Your perfect will in my life.*

## SPIRIT OR FLESH?

*B*EING ABLE TO discern spirits requires you to have a discerning spirit. Deducing, supposing, presuming, or otherwise guessing can be a dangerous exercise. Many times what you think is a spirit is merely the flesh.

Be cautious not to get out of balance in the spiritual realm. The flesh is at enmity with Me. I war against the flesh. Often what you are facing is not a spirit but someone's carnal nature rising up against you. The person's actions may or may not be motivated by a spirit. Always ask Me.

1 John 4:1; 1 Corinthians 12;
1 Thessalonians 5:21

### ✦ PRAYER ✦

*I don't want to play guessing games in the spirit, so I need You to show me what You need me to see. Help me to stay in balance with the Word of God so that I don't open myself up to deception. Increase my ability to discern the spirits.*

## I Will Show You How to Prioritize

**P**EOPLE WILL ALWAYS want more from you than you have to give. They don't understand that there are many standing in line with a want or need. Don't let the demands frustrate you. Learn to recognize My grace on a thing, move in that grace, and trust Me to handle the rest.

You can't please everyone all the time, so don't try. Follow My lead. I will show you how to prioritize the demands, and I will provide the grace you need to meet them. All you must do is receive that grace. Don't let people make you feel guilty that you cannot fulfill their desire.

ROMANS 8:14; GALATIANS 5:18; GALATIANS 5:1

### → PRAYER ←

*Sometimes it feels as if everybody wants a piece of me—but I want to give myself more to You and Your will. Will You teach me to recognize Your grace to move out into service? Will You help me to set right priorities without fear of man?*

## You Are Not Under Attack

*T*oo often I hear you and others say, "I'm under attack," when the enemy is harassing you. That's not a victory mind-set, and you should not go into battle declaring you are under attack. Beloved, the attack is under *you*.

The enemy is under your feet, and you are seated above him—in heavenly places in Christ Jesus. So change your perspective. Yes, the enemy may be attacking you, but you are not *under* his attacks—you are *over* them. Speak and act as if you believe that.

Ephesians 2:4–6; Romans 8:37; 1 John 4:4

### ✦ Prayer ✦

*I repent for not standing in my authority*
*in Christ when the enemy comes against*
*my life. Thank You for reminding me who*
*I am in Christ. Will You strengthen my*
*heart and pour out a spirit of wisdom and*
*revelation in the knowledge of Him?*

*January 6*

## TAKE THE PATHWAY TO PEACE

TRUST IS THE pathway to peace. For there is no fear where trust exists. Love breeds trust, and perfect love casts out all fear. Trust in Me with all your heart and lean not unto your understanding. In all your ways acknowledge Me, and I will direct your steps.

Trust Father to lead and guide you every step of the way into a broad place of blessing where you can come to know Him in a new way. He wants to encounter you today and every day. Trust that He is with you always, and look for His blessings.

1 JOHN 4:18; PSALM 56:3–4; PSALM 13:5

### ✦ PRAYER ✦

*I trust You, Lord. Help me trust You more. I choose to trust You with everything in me. Show me the places of my heart that I am holding back because of fear. I am determined to trust You with all that I am and all that I have. Help me.*

## I DON'T SEE AS MAN SEES

*I* AM EL SHADDAI. I don't see the way man sees. I don't think the way man thinks. I see over, above, and beyond the circumstances that try to weigh you down. So see Me as I am. I am the One who meets your needs, who nourishes your soul, who supplies your heart's desires, who satisfies your hunger and thirst. I am the Lord of abundant blessings, and I will walk with you through the circumstances that try to weigh you down and take you over, above, and beyond where you thought you could go.

GENESIS 17:1; 1 SAMUEL 16:7; MATTHEW 5:6

### → PRAYER ←

*Thank You for being almighty in my life. Thank You for seeing my heart's intentions even when I don't live up to my own standards. Thank You for all of Your promises and all of Your blessings. Help me walk in the fullness of Your plan for me.*

## January 8

### When You Think of Me, Remember These Things

When you think of Me, think of My love for you. It's unfailing. When you think of Me, think of My joy—joy that gives you strength. When you think of Me, think of My peace that can guard your heart and mind in Christ Jesus. When you think of Me, think of My patience.

I don't expect you to be perfect. When you think of Me, think of My gentleness and My goodness. My thoughts toward you are good all the time. When you think of Me, let it inspire faith in your heart, meekness in your character, and self-control in your soul. Think of Me often.

JEREMIAH 29:11; PSALM 119:68; NUMBERS 14:18

### ✦ PRAYER ✦

*You think about me all the time, and that moves my heart. Help me to think of You often. Interrupt my thoughts with Your thoughts. Show me facets of Your character that I need to keep in mind as I walk with You. Remind me of Your greatness.*

## Tap Into the Wellspring of Faith

W HEN THINGS LOOK dark, remember that Jesus is the light. When you feel lost in your trials, remember Jesus is the Way. When your dreams look dead, remember Jesus is the Life. Nothing is impossible to the one who believes, and you have the measure of faith. You have more than mustard-seed faith.

You have faith that overcomes the world. Tap into the wellspring of faith in your spirit, speak the Word out of your mouth, take actions that back up your words, and watch Me move on your behalf. It might not happen today, but it will happen.

JOHN 8:12; JOHN 14:6; MATTHEW 19:26

### → PRAYER ←

*Your words inspire faith in my heart. Faith is rising even now to conquer the giants in my life. Give me wisdom and revelation of Jesus, the Word that became flesh. Give me a steadfast, enduring spirit to hold on to Your Word no matter what circumstances look like.*

## January 10

### DON'T ALLOW YOUR
### FEELINGS TO LEAD YOU

*I*F YOU FEEL discouraged, look to the One who gives you courage. If you feel weak, look to the One who gives you strength. If you feel stressed out, look to the One who gives you perfect peace—supernatural peace that surpasses all understanding and guards your heart and mind. If you feel depressed, look to the One who gives you His very own joy to strengthen you for the battle.

Don't allow your feelings to lead you and guide you. Allow Me to lead you and guide you, and you will live in the truth that sets you free.

2 CORINTHIANS 12:9; JOSHUA 1:9; PSALM 143:7–8

### ✦ PRAYER ✦

*You are always there for me. You are always by my side. No matter how I feel or what comes my way, I can rely on You to speak words of life to my heart. Help me recognize Your presence when my emotions try to take over, and still my soul.*

## SEE YOURSELF IN JESUS

*A*s JESUS IS, so are you in this world. Begin to see yourself as in Him. Clothe yourself with Christ. Look through the lens of His Word. Challenge yourself to cast down imaginations, to resist the devil's onslaught, to battle sickness, to walk in humility, to express love, and to share joy.

When Jesus walked the earth, He submitted Himself to Father and resisted the devil. The result was compassion bestowed on people, the working of miracles, and yes, persecution. It will be the same for you if you submit to Me and live as Jesus lived. But following Me is worth it all.

1 JOHN 4:17; ROMANS 13:14; MATTHEW 16:24

### ⤞ PRAYER ⤝

*I know that I am in Christ. That is my legal position. Help me to understand what that really means in my life. Help me to live and move and have my being in Jesus. Help me to follow Him no matter what people think, say, or do. Help me.*

*January 12*

## Keep On Decreeing and Declaring

You've prayed, petitioned, and offered supplications. You've made intercession and sought Me in prayer. This is all right and in order, but sometimes you need to rise up and take your authority over a thing.

Sometimes after you've prayed, petitioned, offered supplications, and made intercession, you need to decree, declare, and proclaim what you know is Father's will. Keep decreeing, declaring, and proclaiming until you see His will come to pass.

Luke 10:19; Matthew 16:19; 1 John 4:4

### → Prayer →

*Thank You for the authority that You've given me. Help me to discern when to pray, when to bind, when to loose, when to use the right weapon of warfare, and when to let go and believe that You are battling for me. Give me endurance to run the race.*

## YOU WILL SEE SWIFT VICTORY

*T*HERE ARE TIMES when you need to pray fervently for Father to intervene in a situation. There are other times when you need to prophesy to the circumstances and command them to bow to what the Lord has shown you. There are still other times when you need to decree and declare and proclaim the Word of God over yourself or others. Press into Me and get the right prophetic warfare strategy, and you will see swift victory.

EZEKIEL 37:1–14; 2 CORINTHIANS 2:14–15;
JEREMIAH 51:1–7

### ☩ PRAYER ☩

*You always have the battle plans. You always
have the blueprint. You always know the way of
escape and the path to victory. Please help me not
to presume on the spiritual battlefield but to wait
for Your leading and Your strategy for victory.*

## HOLD TIGHTLY TO JESUS

$P$ UT ON YOUR belt of truth. Hold tightly to the truth. Think about things that are true. Stand firmly in the truth. Jesus is the Truth. His Word is truth. What I speak to your heart is truth. The truth that you know—really know—sets you free. Don't allow anyone to lead you away from the truth about Jesus, about yourself, about your calling. Dream-killers and deceivers abound in this hour. False friends will deceive you in the name of truth if you don't guard your heart. Hold tightly to the truth.

EPHESIANS 6:14; JOHN 8:32; PROVERBS 4:23

### ⇥ PRAYER ⇤

*Your words are truth that taste sweet to my soul.*
*Thank You for sharing Your truth with my heart.*
*Help me to be a lover of the truth, holding fast*
*to the truth and discerning and destroying all*
*deception and lies that try to make me stumble.*

## Turn the Other Cheek

**D**on't retaliate. Don't swap railing for railing. Don't move in the same wrong spirit that's moving against you. Don't stoop to the enemy's level. Don't mistake as your enemy the person who is plaguing you with problems you don't need.

The devil is your enemy, and you will defeat him by walking in love, by turning the other cheek, by moving in the opposite spirit. Defy the devil by rising up in My love and waiting on Father's justice. It's a process, beloved, but it's guaranteed to produce the outcome you and I both desire for you. Agree with the Word, and let's get started.

Ephesians 6:12; Ephesians 5:2; Matthew 5:39

### ❖ Prayer ❖

*Thank You for reminding me who my real enemy is. Thank You for reminding me of the Sermon on the Mount. Help me to walk in this truth. Help me not to take my own vengeance. Please give me the grace to submit to the process.*

## January 16

### REMEMBER MERCY

*J*AMES WROTE THESE words that you need to remember: mercy triumphs over judgment. I inspired him to write those words for the generations because I know that human nature is to be critical and judgmental—and even to be self-condemning. When someone is judging you, don't criticize him for operating without mercy. Don't answer back against the accusations the accuser of the brethren is hurling at you. Remember that mercy triumphs over judgment, and show mercy, love, and grace instead because your critics need to see Jesus alive in you.

JAMES 2:13; LUKE 6:36; MATTHEW 5:7

### → PRAYER ←

*You are so merciful. You are so full of grace.*
*I want to be like You. I want to be quick*
*to forgive, gracious, loving, patient, and*
*kind even when people are not treating*
*me in this manner. Help me receive Your*
*mercy so that I have mercy to give others.*

## I Will Give You the Words to Speak

*I* know you don't like confrontations. Most people don't. They are uncomfortable, but you don't need to shrink back for fear of hurting someone or for fear of a blow-up. Don't fear confrontations when they are necessary—and many times there's no other way to address an ongoing situation.

Don't get into imaginations beforehand about how the confrontation will play out either. Approach the confrontation in a godly manner, and I will give you wise words of truth to speak with grace and life to resolve the matter.

2 Timothy 1:7; 2 Corinthians 10:5; Luke 21:15

### ✤ Prayer ✤

*I would rather suffer than fail to do Father's will. And sometimes that suffering means confronting things I should not tolerate because they defy the Word. Give me grace and strength and peace when I have to confront these people and situations.*

## January 18

## I Will Show You When to Rest

*P*EOPLE WILL ALWAYS come to challenge you to step out of the role Father has given you. Even well-meaning people will tell you that you are going to burn out if you don't slow down. They will tell you that you don't have to try so hard. They will tell you that you can lower your standards.

Don't listen to them. Listen to Me. I will show you when to rest. I will show you what to let go. I will show you what is necessary. Don't compromise your standards or your calling. Recall your place in Christ and stand for what He has put in your heart to do.

ROMANS 8:14; ISAIAH 30:21; JOHN 16:13

### → PRAYER ←

*Thank You for this promise. I want to do all that You're calling me to do, but I need wisdom about when to rest and when to run. Help me discern Your timing. Please give me strength and power to run this race with endurance to the end.*

## Jesus Wants to Be Your Rock

W HEN OLD ENEMIES rise up against you—and the enemy does come back around to tempt you in different seasons—remember that Jesus is your rock, your fortress, and your deliverer. He is the strength of your life and the salvation of your soul. He is your defender and vindicator. He is your warrior, and He is warring on your behalf. Remember, you already have the victory in Christ, even when Christians are the ones who are mocking and persecuting you. Trust in Jesus. He wants to be your rock. Let Him.

LUKE 4:13; PSALM 18:2; PSALM 27

### ✦ PRAYER ✦

*Jesus is my everything. Thank You for always pointing the way back to Christ, my risen Savior. Help me remember these words in the heat of the battle, in the fiery trial, and on the bad days. Help me to declare these truths in the midst of the storm.*

## January 20

### JESUS UNDERSTANDS YOU INTIMATELY

Sometimes people—even people who genuinely love you and want the best for you—will misunderstand you. Jesus knows the truth. Sometimes it's not worth explaining how they've misunderstood because they just *can't* understand, as much as they want to.

Don't let that bother you. And don't strive for understanding from men. Know that you have a High Priest who understands you intimately. Know that I understand. I am your comforter. I am your advocate. Turn to Me, and I will release you from the pain of being sorely misunderstood.

1 Corinthians 2:14; Hebrews 12:3;
Philippians 4:6–7

### ✦ PRAYER ✦

*Being misunderstood can be painful. Having the motives of my heart judged—especially when my motives are pure—really stings. Yet I know Jesus understands how I feel. Help me not to dwell on the pain of misunderstandings when they occur.*

## Stop and Pray When Pressure Comes

When you begin to feel overwhelmed by circumstances, stop and pray. I know it's tempting to press through with all the responsibilities and deadlines. But be intentional. Change your scenery. Step outside. Prayer will offer you the perspective you're looking for.

Slow down and think about Jesus. His peace will rise up in your heart, and the power that raised Christ from the dead will grace you with whatever you need to keep running the race. Taking ten minutes to pray could change the course of your day. Try it.

1 Thessalonians 5:17; Luke 18:1;
Matthew 21:22

### ✦ Prayer ✦

*Prayer is my lifeline, but when the deadlines
come—when the pressure comes—sometimes
I forget to lift up my voice in prayer. Please
prompt me. Please help me cultivate a lifestyle of
praying immediately when the pressure comes.*

## January 22

### GUARD YOUR COMMUNICATIONS

THE DEVIL IS the prince of the power of the air, so it's no surprise that he likes to work in the realm of your communication with family, friends, and coworkers. Remember this: lack of communication can open the door for the enemy as much untimely or poor communication. Lack of communication can lead to people around you having imaginations, taking on attitudes, and even committing actions that are not pleasing to God. Learn to communicate and communicate well. Don't presume or assume. I will help you.

EPHESIANS 2:2; EPHESIANS 4:29; 2 TIMOTHY 2:16

### ✦ PRAYER ✦

*Help me to season my speech with grace. Help my words release life to all those who hear them. Let people hear Your love in my voice with every word I utter. Place a guard over my mouth that I might not speak rashly.*

## STICK CLOSE TO MY WORDS

STICK TO YOUR godly convictions. Stick to your biblical principles. Refuse to compromise the Word. Determine to meditate on Scripture day and night and to do all that it says so you can find good success. Another path toward your goals may seem expedient. It's easy enough to compromise in this day and age. But blessed are you when you purpose in your heart to walk in the law of God. Blessings will chase you down and overtake you.

JOHN 14:15; JOSHUA 1:8; DEUTERONOMY 28:2

### ✦ PRAYER ✦

*I refuse to compromise the Word of God. I refuse to neglect studying the Bible. Help me set aside anything that is getting in the way of my pursuit of the truth. Help me stand strong and bold when the temptation to compromise what You've said arises.*

## January 24

### FATHER ALWAYS LEADS YOU INTO TRIUMPH

*W*HEN YOUR ARMS are heavy from holding your shield of faith, when you are tempted to lay down your sword, when you have lost your shoes of peace, and when your helmet of salvation seems shaky, then tighten the belt of truth around your waist.

The enemy of your soul spews lies to convince you that you'll never win the battle. But the truth is, Father always leads you into triumph in Christ. You are in Him. Move and live and have your being in Him. Victory belongs to you.

EPHESIANS 6:12–17; JOHN 8:44;
2 CORINTHIANS 2:14

### ⇢ PRAYER ⇠

*I believe the truth that You have shared with my heart. I reject the lies from the wicked one, who has been lying from the beginning. Give me the strength to keep fighting the good fight of faith. Give me the strength to stand and withstand.*

## You Can Rejoice in These Realities

*L*ook up. Look up. Your redemption draws near. You're closer than you think to eternity. Rejoice in your right standing with Father. Rejoice that your name is written in the Lamb's Book of Life. Rejoice in your fellowship with Me. Rejoice in the reality that you have a future and a hope. Rejoice in the knowledge that you are loved and cherished. Rejoice in the good days and the bad, and remember that this world is not your home. Eternity awaits.

Luke 21:28; Luke 10:20; Hebrews 13:14

### ✣ Prayer ✣

*You've given me so much in which to rejoice. I will rejoice in all of this and more. I will rejoice in You. Show me new facets of Christ's beauty, Your love, and Father's kingdom so that I can continually rejoice in new revelations about who You are.*

## January 26

### I Have Put My Dreams in Your Heart

*I* AM THE ONE who put My dream in your heart. I am the One who gave you the desire to heal the sick. I am the One who draws you to the secret place to cry out for the dreams and desires that I have put in your heart. So continue drawing near to Me, and I will continue drawing near to you.

I will help you manifest your purpose and walk in your destiny. I will show you what to let go of and what to grab hold of. I will help you align your will perfectly with Mine and release My gifts in faith.

MATTHEW 10:8; JAMES 4:8; 1 CORINTHIANS 12:31

#### ✦ PRAYER ✦

*Draw me close to You so I can feel Your love and hear Your heartbeat. You have given me dreams for my life that are part of my purpose in Christ. Please give me the wisdom to walk out of things that are holding me back and into Father's perfect will.*

## Always Look to Me

Stay focused on Me and only Me. Your detractors will come whispering accusations. Look to Me. Your adversaries will come trumpeting lies. Look to Me. Your friends will come with words that cannot comfort you. Look to Me. Your family will misunderstand you. Look to Me. Some will hate you for Christ's sake. Look to Me. Father will vindicate you in due time. Look to Me in the meantime.

John 15:18; Isaiah 50:8; Psalm 4:2–4

### ✦ Prayer ✦

*There are so many distractions in the world. There are so many voices demanding my attention. Help me to sort through it all. Help me to be still and listen for Your leading. Help me not to take matters into my own hands.*

## January 28

### RISE UP IN JESUS'S NAME!

STOP TOLERATING THE enemy's lies! Break every word curse that's coming against you in the name of Jesus. Bind the witchcraft that's attacking your mind and body. Refuse to bow to the enemy's spiritual-warfare tactics.

Rise up now in the name of your Lord. Resist the devil, and remember you are not wrestling against flesh and blood. Rest for your soul is available, but many times you have to labor to enter that rest. If you keep pressing into Me to obtain the peace that passes all understanding, you will find the still waters you're looking for.

MATTHEW 11:28; HEBREWS 4:11; PSALM 23:2

#### ✦ PRAYER ✦

*Sometimes I tolerate things that You've called me to stand against because I don't want to stir up a hornet's nest with people. Help me find the rest You've promised. Help me find the peace that passes all understanding that Jesus offers me.*

# Be Careful Whom You Listen To

**B**E CAREFUL WHOM you listen to. Be careful what you look at. Be careful what you agree with. For in this hour there are many voices competing for your attention, and they are not all righteous. There are many dreams and visions to follow, but they don't all come from My heart. There are many doctrines and arguments, but they are not all grounded in truth. Stick close to Me. Listen for My voice amid the chaos and seek My face in the midst of the darkness, and you will know what is real and what is false.

PSALM 32:8–9; PSALM 119:105; MARK 4:24

## ✦ PRAYER ✦

*Thank You for always warning me—and for always leading and guiding me into truth. I will listen for Your voice and Your voice alone. Help me to tune in to what You are doing and saying every step of the way and every day of my life.*

## January 30

### WELCOME ME ALL THE WAY IN

WELCOME ME. WELCOME ME into parts of your life that cause you worry and stress. Welcome Me into parts of your soul that are fearful or sorrowful. Welcome Me into parts of your heart that are not fully submitted to Me. Welcome Me into your mind, will, and emotions. Welcome Me into your family and into your workplace. Welcome Me into every part of who you are, and I will fill you with all that I am. I will not come uninvited. Welcome Me.

1 John 4:12; John 20:22; 1 John 3:24

#### → PRAYER ←

*I welcome You. I welcome Your presence. I welcome Your teaching. I welcome Your leading and Your guiding. I welcome Your wisdom and Your conviction. Help me stay open to everything You want to share and everything You want to do in my life.*

## LET ME HELP YOU

**W**HY WON'T YOU let Me help you? Sometimes I watch you run from here to there and back and forth and wear yourself out. Why won't you let Me help you? Your consuming zeal for My house blesses My heart, but let Me give you the grace, strength, wisdom, and strategies you need. Exchange the strength of your will for My grace, and then running from here to there and back and forth won't wear you out. Try it and you'll see the difference in how your days go.

JOHN 14:26; ROMANS 8:26, HEBREWS 4:16

### ✦ PRAYER ✦

*I need Your help—more than I know. And I want Your help. Show me the areas where I am too quick to move without Your leading or too quick to speak without Your prompting. Help me to truly receive the aid You so want to give me.*

# February

For I am persuaded that neither death nor life,
neither angels nor principalities nor powers, neither things present nor things to come, neither height nor depth, nor any other created
thing, shall be able to separate us from the love
of God, which is in Christ Jesus our Lord.

—ROMANS 8:38–39

## Behold Jesus at All Times

Behold the Lamb of God who took away the sin of the world. Now, behold Him as the One who took away your sins. Father doesn't expect you to be perfect. He expects you to mature in Christ by beholding the Sinless One who loves you so much. He expects you to exercise your faith to walk in His Word. He expects you to love Him, love others, and love yourself. So focus on Him instead of your mistakes and failures. He is there when you fall. Behold Him.

John 1:29; Romans 8:5; Revelation 21:4

### ⤞ Prayer ⤝

*I long to behold the beauty of my beautiful Savior day and night. Thank You for always pointing me to Jesus. Thank You for revealing more and more of Him to my heart. Help me to grasp a measure of the infinite grace and mercy He carries.*

## February 2

### MY FAVOR RESTS UPON YOU

*Y*ou don't have to try to win My favor. You already have My favor. You already have My approval. You already have My blessing. You already have My heart. What you really need is a greater revelation that My favor rests upon you; that My goodness and mercy follow you every day of your life; that I love you with all My heart, all My soul, all My mind, and all My strength. Just be with Me. That's all I want right now.

Psalm 84:11; Ephesians 1:11; Proverbs 3:1–4

### → PRAYER ←

*I rejoice in Your favor. The favor of God puts me over the top. Help me not to strive for favor when it already belongs to me. Show me what Christ really offered me through His victory at Calvary. That's all I want right now.*

## I Will Never Let You Down

*I* LOVE TO HEAR you pray because it demonstrates your dependence on Father. I want you to lean and depend on Us and not on your own understanding. I want you to acknowledge Us in all your ways. We want to direct your steps. It's your humility of heart and confidence in Christ that allow Me the freedom in your life to move how I want to move, even when you don't see the path ahead. Continue depending on Us. We won't let you down—ever.

PSALM 5:3; PROVERBS 3:5–6; PSALM 37:5

### ✦ PRAYER ✦

*I am completely and utterly dependent upon*
*You. Help me not to rise up in my emotions,*
*my mind, or my flesh and move ahead of*
*You. Teach me to maintain an attitude of*
*dependence, and give me the grace of humility.*

## Give Honor to Whom Honor Is Due

*H*onor those around you just like you would honor Me, even when they are not behaving in a way that is worthy of honor. When you love those around you even when they behave in a way that contradicts love, you are acting like your Father who is in heaven. Give honor to whom honor is due and act honorably toward those who don't seem to deserve honor. In doing so, you may draw them to Christ. It's part of walking in love.

Romans 12:9–13; 1 Peter 2:17–19; Romans 13:7

### → Prayer ←

*Your wisdom amazes me. You are no respecter of persons. You intended for all of us to honor one another. Help me to show honor—even to give double honor to those who labor in the kingdom. Show me ways to demonstrate honor to whom it is due.*

## Bind Yourself to Me

*W*HEN YOU BIND yourself to Me, the things that oppose My will in your life—sins, fleshly lusts, and even demons—cannot bind themselves to you. When you cling to Me, nothing can by any means harm you. When you abide in My love, when you abide in the Word, the things that tempt you to stray from My heart cannot abide with you or in you. Bind yourself to Me, and I, the Spirit of truth, will set you free from every snare of the enemy and every carnal desire. When you bind yourself to Me, you'll spend a lot less time binding the devil.

DEUTERONOMY 10:20; JOSHUA 23:8; PSALM 63:8

### ✦ PRAYER ✦

*I will cling to You even when my mind tries to wander to toxic thoughts. I will cling to You even when the enemy is tempting my soul to turn the other way. Give me a determined heart to cling to You, abide in You, and walk in Your truth.*

## February 6

### PRESS INTO THE FULLNESS
### OF FATHER'S PLANS

*Y*ou are on My mind. You are in My heart. I am watching over you. Not a moment goes by when I am not thinking about you and Father's good plans for you and how I can help you walk toward your destiny in Christ. I am interceding for you. Jesus is interceding for you. Father's good pleasure is to give you the kingdom. So now press into the fullness of His plans for you. It's worth any sacrifice you have to make to get there. Take My word for it.

PSALM 139:17; JEREMIAH 29:11; ROMANS 8:34

### ✦ PRAYER ✦

*Who am I that You are mindful of me? You so committed to praying with and for me because of the kind intent of Your will. Please give me greater insight into Your heart as I draw close to You day and night. I want to know You more.*

## NO PERFORMANCE IS NECESSARY

*I*T GRIEVES My heart to see you wallow in guilt and stew in condemnation over your mistakes or your frustrations about your performance. Father is looking for worshippers, not performers. Jesus made a way for you to approach Father's throne of grace to receive mercy for your mistakes and sins. No performance is necessary— just meekness and repentance and a heart that seeks obedience. Just seek Me.

EPHESIANS 4:30; ROMANS 8:1; JOHN 4:24

### ✦ PRAYER ✦

*Religion teaches me to perform, to strive, to prove myself. But Your grace demands nothing but a heart aiming at obedience. Thank You for Your great grace. Help me to be quick to receive the grace and mercy to help in time of need.*

*February 8*

## LET'S WORK TOGETHER

*Y*OU NEED TO put all the thoughts that contradict the Word of God out of your mind—every single one of them. I cannot do that for you, as much as I want to. I can help you discern those wrong thoughts. I can remind you of what the Word says. It's up to you to remain close enough to Me to hear My warnings. It's up to you to cast down those vain imaginations and wrong thoughts. I'm doing My part, and I'll help you do your part. Let's work together.

HEBREWS 4:12; JOHN 14:26; 1 CORINTHIANS 3:9

### ⟶ PRAYER ⟵

*I hear You loud and clear. I will prize Your loving voice over all others that come with lies to tear me down. Thank You for training my ear to hear and my eyes to see. Help me sharpen my discernment so that I can quickly cast down what is not of You.*

## KEEP THE VISION BEFORE YOU

*T*HAT VOICE YOU hear telling you that you can't do what I've told you to do is not Me. Why would I call you into this new thing and fail to supply the grace, resources, and connections you need to complete your assignment? Shut out the enemy's voice and meditate on what I've told you. As you do, you will receive more revelation on how to move forward, as well as the courage to do it. Keep the vision before you no matter what you encounter, and you will overcome all.

PHILIPPIANS 4:19; PSALM 29:4; 1 SAMUEL 30:8

### → PRAYER ←

*You are faithful to supply everything I need
to do what You've called me to do. Every
thought contrary to that truth must be
obliterated in my mind. Help me to meditate
on Your promises and get Your truth in
my spirit so it can renew my mind.*

## February 10

### PRESS PAST THE DISTRACTIONS

My thoughts are higher than your thoughts, and My ways are higher than your ways. But you can see many things the way I see them if You ask Me to open the eyes of your heart. You can receive My wisdom if you have an ear to hear what the Spirit of God says. Be careful what you look at and how you hear. I am willing to share My thoughts with you. I am willing to show you My ways if you are willing to truly see. Press past the distractions around you and seek My face, and you will see Me.

Isaiah 55:9; Ephesians 1:8; 1 John 2:15

### → PRAYER ←

*Please give me an ear to hear everything that You are trying to communicate to me. Please teach me Your ways and share with me Your thoughts, and give me a determination to press past the distractions that dull my hearing.*

## Stop Meditating on Your Mistakes

*Y*ou have to stop considering past sin and meditating on past mistakes during our time of fellowship together. Father will not reject a broken and repentant heart, and I bless those with a contrite spirit. Father chose long ago not to remember your past sins, and He does not meditate on your past mistakes after you repent. Take My hand and walk with Me in the present toward your future. Forget what lies behind. Your future is brighter than the darkness in your past.

1 John 1:9; Psalm 51:17; Isaiah 43:25

### ✢ Prayer ✢

*The enemy tries to use my past mistakes like a magnet, but I will not let those memories draw me backward. Give me the strength to resist the temptation to think about things I can't go back and change. Help me set my heart on You.*

## PRIZE MY WORDS

*I*F YOU PRIZE the Word of God above the word of man, then you will find peace, provision, and power manifesting in your life in ways you could not have anticipated. Prize My voice above the many other voices competing for your agreement and you will advance more rapidly. Prize my instruction above the vain imaginations that you are tempted to speak out in times of distress. Prize my voice over the reasoning of your own soul. My Word will not return to Me void. It will accomplish what I intend it to do. Prize it.

2 TIMOTHY 3:16; PROVERBS 4:20–22;
MATTHEW 24:35

### ✦ PRAYER ✦

*Father's Word is light and life. His Word is
purified seven times. Help me to make His Word
an even bigger priority in my life so that my
mind will be renewed day by day, and I will not
only hear His Word but also do it and be blessed.*

## I Want to Use You as an Agent of Love

*I* want to mature you in love. I want you to understand and experience My love at a deeper level—then at an even deeper level. The world is full of hurting people who can be difficult to love unless you are overflowing with a revelation of My love to you and for you—and those around you. I want to use you as an agent of love to draw people to My heart. So receive My love, love yourself, and then commit to loving other people. It will radically change your life and impact those around you.

1 Corinthians 16:14; Matthew 22:36–40; 1 John 4:8

### ☩ Prayer ☩

*At the end of the day, it's all about love. Love is the foundation of Your kingdom and the motive of Your heart. Help me to walk in love. Help me to pour out Your perfect love to people in need. Show me how to love well.*

## February 14

### RECEIVE FATHER'S LOVE FOR YOU

*I*T'S MORE THAN a song. Father loves you with all of His heart, all of His soul, all of His strength, and all of His might. He loves you unconditionally. He delights in you. It's not about what you can do for Him or even what He can do through you. It's about His heart for you. You are His unique creation. You are the apple of His eye. You ravish His heart with just one glance in His direction. He loves you with an unfaltering, unfailing, undying love. What would happen if you really believed these words? Only believe.

JOHN 3:16; 1 JOHN 4:19; ROMANS 8:38–39

#### → PRAYER ←

*I believe. Help me believe more deeply and more fully. A revelation of Your perfect love will cast out everything that doesn't belong in my life. Give me a stronger revelation of that perfect love so I can love You more.*

## Allow Your Soul to Enter My Rest

Sometimes you wonder why you feel so worn out even after you rest your body. The reason for this is the weight of your soul. When you choose to carry burdens in your own strength and forget to cast your cares on Jesus, the load becomes too heavy for any man to bear. So rest your physical body; physical rest is certainly important. But allow your soul to enter My rest and you will be truly refreshed in spirit, soul, and body.

Galatians 6:9; Exodus 33:14; Mark 6:31

### ✦ Prayer ✦

*I don't want to refuse Your invitation to rest, yet I realize that often I do. Help me to discern when I am carrying cares that I need to cast on You. Show me how to balance my life with work and rest so I can walk in Your refreshing presence throughout the day.*

## YOUR APPRECIATION
## ATTRACTS MY KINDNESS

*I*T BLESSES My heart to hear you praise and give thanks for Father's goodness. The overwhelming gratitude that you express for what Christ has done in and through you brings Us joy and causes Us to want to do even more for you. Your appreciation attracts Our attention and Our kindness. I have something to tell you: *you haven't seen anything yet.* This is just the beginning. So stay grateful and stay ready because We have so much more to walk through together.

1 THESSALONIANS 5:18; PSALM 107:1;
EPHESIANS 5:20

### ⇨ PRAYER ⇦

*I am grateful—eternally grateful for what
You have done, what You are doing, and
what You are going to do in my life. I don't
deserve any of it, but I want to receive all
of it for Your glory. Help me to receive
and stay thankful on this journey.*

## Choose to Let Faith Arise

*L*ET FAITH ARISE in your heart. It will if you will let it. For Father has given every person the measure of faith. You already have all the faith you need to believe for the miracles and breakthroughs you will need as you walk through life. Let faith arise by pushing the doubts, reasoning, vain imaginations, and ungodly emotions out of your soul. Let faith arise by rejecting any thoughts or ideas that are out of line with My will. Choose to let faith arise.

MATTHEW 21:22; HEBREWS 11:1;
2 CORINTHIANS 5:7

### ✦ PRAYER ✦

*You are so faithful that You've even given me the faith I need to receive from Your heart. Show me where I need to build myself up in faith. Help me to release my faith with my prayers. Teach me how to use my faith in a way that gives You glory.*

## February 18

### EMBRACE THIS DIVINE EXCHANGE

*I*'D LIKE TO do a divine exchange with you. You give me your stress, and I'll give you My peace. You give me your frustration, and I'll give you My grace. You give me your sorrow and grief, and I'll give you My joy. You give me your fear, and I'll give you My love. Now hear this: the divine exchange was made at Calvary. Jesus already gave it all. Just tap in to what belongs to you.

ROMANS 6:13; ISAIAH 61:3; JOHN 16:15

### → PRAYER ←

*I'll take You up on Your divine exchange.
I want to know everything that belongs
to me in the spirit realm. Help me to
grab hold of the revelation that Jesus
died so that I might be healthy, whole,
prosperous, peaceful, joyous, and more.*

## I Know an Easier Way Through

*I*f you need help, just ask Me. I am right here. I am your helper. I am standing by. I am as close as your next prayer. Why not ask for help instead of running yourself ragged, wearing yourself out, and walking in circles? Believe Me, I know an easier way through. I can show you the way over or around. I know a better way. I'll show you if you ask Me. I don't want to watch you struggle for no reason when I can give you a more strategic route through your days. Try Me. I won't let you down. My grace is available to you.

John 14:26; Luke 4:14; Romans 8:11

### ✦ Prayer ✦

*You know all things. I need to lean on You more.*
*Please prompt me, check me, and show me when*
*I am not acknowledging You. Don't let me get*
*too far out there beyond Your grace. Show me*
*solutions to my problems and give me Your grace.*

# February 20

## Bless Those Who Mistreat You

Despite the many times you've read and quoted Ephesians 6:12, you sometimes still fall into the trap of viewing people who mistreat you as enemies. People are not your enemies. As for their actions, the devil is influencing their behavior at times, and at other times their carnal nature is taking over.

Either way, you're not really wrestling against flesh and blood—and flesh and blood is not wrestling against you. Remember what Paul said: "Bless those who persecute you" (Rom. 12:14). I'm telling you to bless those who mistreat you and to forgive them.

Proverbs 11:25–26; Romans 12:14; 1 Peter 3:9

### → Prayer ←

*Thank You for reminding me. It sure seems sometimes like I'm wrestling against people. Help me to see what's going on behind the scenes in the spirit realm. Help me to discern the real enemy. Show me how to bless always.*

## I Am Your Way of Escape

Sometimes you look for a way of escape— and sometimes you need one. But sometimes you look for a way of escape when escaping is not My best plan for you. You may escape for a moment or two by letting off steam with a friend, eating too much, or sleeping too long, but the devil is in the excess. Father is faithful to provide you a way of escape in every temptation and trial. Walk close to Me. Remember, I am your way of escape, and I am always available to draw you away when you call upon Me.

1 Corinthians 10:13; Luke 21:36; Isaiah 43:2

### ❖ Prayer ❖

*Sometimes I feel like David when he wrote in Psalm 55:6 that he wished he could just fly away from his troubles. Life is not easy sometimes, but nothing is impossible with You. Give me an enduring heart and a steadfast spirit. Draw me into Your presence when I am looking for a way of escape.*

## February 22

### LOOK AT THE BIG PICTURE

*L*OOK AT THE big picture. When you focus on the minor details of your life for too long, you see everything that is wrong. It's OK to look at your life and seek to make changes that will bring you closer to Father's heart. But don't make mountains out of molehills. Look at the big picture. Look at how far you've come, how much you've learned, and how much you've changed. I am changing you from glory to glory. Don't get bogged down in what the enemy wants to show you about yourself.

HEBREWS 2:1; COLOSSIANS 1:16;
2 CORINTHIANS 3:18

### → PRAYER ←

*Would You please give me Your perspective on my life? Show me what I am not seeing. Help me look past what the enemy wants to show me and what my unrenewed mind sees and give me heaven-colored glasses.*

## Do This When You Feel Weary

Sometimes you don't fully recognize the level of resistance coming against you because you're so determined to press into My will. I love that about you. Wisdom dictates that when you grow weary, you must slow down long enough to discern the assignment against your soul in order to prevent the enemy's seeds from taking root while you continue plowing ahead. If you are growing weary, it's a sign that you are either moving outside My grace or you are moving into enemy territory. Take a moment to ask Me what is going on so that you can pull back or press in at the right time.

Revelation 2:3; Hebrews 12:3; Psalm 62:1

### → Prayer ←

*I don't think I even want to know the level of resistance I'm facing, but I do want to know more about You. Help me to stay focused on Your heart, Your plan, and Your purposes. Strengthen me to press past what's pressing against me— or to wait until You show me what to do.*

## February 24

## I WILL SHOW YOU WHERE TO GO

WHERE DO YOU go from here? I will surely show you. Just keep yielding to Me. Just keep following Me. Just keep looking at Me and for Me and to Me. Just keep listening to Me and really hearing Me. Just keep walking with Me and talking with Me and praying with Me to your Father who is in heaven. He's a good Father and knows how to give good gifts to you—and He wants to. Your Father in heaven has plans for you beyond what you can imagine. I know where you go from here, and I'm leading and guiding you in Father's will.

PROVERBS 28:26; PSALM 143:10; MATTHEW 7:11

### → PRAYER ←

*Holy Spirit, you know everything and see everything. You are full of wisdom and life—and I know You are committed to me. Give me an undivided heart that I might chase after Your presence and follow You everywhere You lead me.*

## COME CLOSER NOW

*I* WANT YOU. I want all of you. I want to be everything you need. I am offering all that I am to you. All you have to do is accept My love invitation. I have gifts for you. And most of all, I have an unending, unwavering, unrelenting love for you. Come closer now. Lean into Me. Give it all to Me. Give yourself to Me. I am yours. All that I have is available to you. This is an open invitation for more and more. Will you RSVP?

PROVERBS 23:26; ROMANS 12:1;
1 CORINTHIANS 6:19–20

### ✦ PRAYER ✦

*I accept Your love invitation and am willing to lay down my own agenda and desires and pick up Your agenda and desires. Your way is better than my way, and Your love is greater than my love. I give You all of me.*

## February 26

### LET IT ALL GO

Some days you are too concerned about so many things. You remind me of Martha, running around in your busyness, finding frustration at every turn, meeting with disappointment because others aren't helping you, and complaining and grumbling about what other people have left you to do. Why not let go of all the concerns, frustrations, disappointments, and complaints and just sit at the feet of Jesus for a while? Some days you could learn a lot from Mary.

Luke 10:38–42; Psalm 27; John 13:23–25

### ⇢ PRAYER ⇠

*Thank You for pointing this out. I know You loved both Martha and Mary, but Mary chose the good part. Help me balance the Martha and Mary within me. Help me learn what Mary knew when she chose what would not be taken from her.*

## I Will Show Myself
## Strong in Your Life

Don't be apprehensive. Don't worry. Don't fret. Don't fear. Don't I always warn you before you head off in a wrong direction? Don't I always give you a way of escape? Haven't I promised to pour out My wisdom? Don't I always keep all My promises? Am I a man that I should lie? Am I a son of man that I should repent? Trust Me. I will show Myself strong in your life. I am the True and Faithful One.

2 Timothy 2:13; Psalm 37:8;
2 Corinthians 1:20

### ✦ Prayer ✦

*You are mighty. You are strong. You are faithful, and You are true. Help me to trust You with all my heart. Help me to truly believe what You whisper in my ear. Teach me how to extend my faith to receive all of Father's promises.*

## Get Your Mind off Your Problems

So much of what you dwell on is insignificant in eternity. Your mind wanders and wonders and ponders and reasons and wrangles over minor matters that don't really matter.

What would your life be like if you took all the time you spend thinking about the minor issues and thought about Me and My love for you? How would your emotions change if you took your mind off your problems and put your mind on the Prince of Peace? Are you willing to find out?

Romans 8:5–6; Philippians 4:8; Galatians 5:1

### ◆ Prayer ◆

*Yes, I am willing to find out what my life would be like if I thought about what is good, pure, lovely, and acceptable. Help me grab hold of my mind when it begins to wander away from Father's Word. Show me how the enemy is distracting my heart.*

## I Am Your Protection

*I* AM YOUR PROTECTION. You don't have to protect yourself from your enemies. Just trust Me. I will deliver you out of their hands if you fall into their snares. I will vindicate you with My truth. I will prepare a table before you in the presence of those who have wrongly accused you. They will see the folly of their ways. Your part is to let Me protect you. Vengeance is Mine. I will repay.

PSALM 91; PSALM 23:4–5; PSALM 125:2

### → PRAYER ←

*You are my protector. Show me when I am
coming out from under Your protection
and trying to guard my own heart and take
my own vengeance. Help me wait upon
Father's vindication and avoid the snare
of taking matters into my own hands.*

# March

Ask for rain from the LORD during the season of
the latter spring rains. And the LORD will make
the storm winds; and He will give them showers
of rain; all will have vegetation in the field.

—ZECHARIAH 10:1

## STOP DWELLING ON THE DRAMA

WHEN EVERYTHING COMES out in the open, the dust has settled on the drama, and you see clearly that you made the right decision, let it go. Stop dwelling on the drama.

Be grateful that you discerned My will in the matter, that you saw the signs I was showing you, that you followed My leading and guidance into the truth in which you stand. Be grateful, learn the lesson, and move on. If you dwell there, you'll miss the next thing I am trying to do. If you glean wisdom from the experience, you'll come up higher.

PHILIPPIANS 1:9–10; HEBREWS 5:14;
PROVERBS 3:1–6

### → PRAYER ←

*I don't want to get stuck in the mud called drama. Drama will always come knocking at the door of my mind. Help me not to answer. Teach me how to stay prayerful when I can't avoid the drama, and show me what I can learn so I will grow in wisdom.*

## March 2

### KEEP ADVANCING IN YOUR KINGDOM PURPOSE

*I*F YOU THINK you will advance without enemy resistance, think again. But don't think about the possibility of retreating when I am leading you into My will. Don't think about the possibility of pulling back when I've called you to war.

Don't give thought to giving up. Keep executing Father's plan for your life. Keep advancing in your kingdom purpose. Stay focused on the outcome; it's a victorious outcome. I am with you.

MATTHEW 11:12; JOEL 3:9; DEUTERONOMY 20:4

### ✦ PRAYER ✦

*I am determined to follow You into battle—to run to the battle line. Give me the grace to back up that determination so I will not retreat when the war rages. Help me stay focused on the victory Father has promised me.*

## Don't Move Too Fast

Sometimes things can look like My will, sound like My will, feel like My will, smell like My will, and taste like My will—but they are not My will. Don't move too fast. Don't go by what your natural senses show you or what people tell you. Well-meaning people can give you poor advice. Facts can be deceiving. People can be deceiving. Your own heart can be deceiving. Pray it through and wait on Me. I will never deceive you.

Romans 12:2; Jeremiah 17:9; Micah 7:7

### ✦ Prayer ✦

*What wisdom You share. You know I have
a tendency to move too fast sometimes.
Help me to discern rightly where You are
leading me. Help me stay on pace with Your
plans. Teach me to resist the temptation
to move beyond Your great grace.*

## March 4

## I Will Lead You Into Times of Rest

WHEN YOU ARE tired, rest. This is not a great mystery of Father's kingdom. It's a clear command He has given for your own good, just as every other command is intended for your good.

If you follow Me—really follow Me—I will lead you into times of rest and times of refreshing, not only for your weary soul but also for your weary body. Don't resist My unction to rest. Don't resist My leading you beside still waters. You need this.

PSALM 23:2–3; PROVERBS 3:7–8; ISAIAH 44:3

### ✦ PRAYER ✦

*Your wisdom is so simple yet so profound.*
*Help me to apply it with childlike faith.*
*Show me how to discern Your unction to*
*rest so that I am not running ahead of You.*
*Take me to those still waters when I need*
*refreshing for my spirit, soul, and body.*

# DON'T LINGER ON DISAPPOINTMENTS

*D*ISAPPOINTMENTS ARE BOUND to come— and they will go. They will fade away unless you linger on them. Life is full of situations, circumstances, and events that don't go the way you hoped. But if you decide to trust Me with your disappointments instead of dwelling on them, then you will gain strength and perspective that will help you move forward with confidence that I am working it all together for your good. Trust Me. I'm on your side.

ROMANS 8:28; GENESIS 50:20; PSALM 112:7

### ⁖ PRAYER ⁖

*I've lived long enough to know this, yet
disappointment still stings. Still, I know
that Father really is working everything
together for good because I love Him and
am called according to His purpose. Please
help me to stand on that promise.*

# March 6

## Don't Answer Back

Sometimes you just have to remain silent, even when people are throwing you under the bus, painting you with the wrong brush and the wrong color, and otherwise manipulating perception of you. When you let Father deal with these situations, you will come out smelling like a rose and having greater authority in the spirit than you previously had. No matter how wrong people are, no matter how hot the fire, no matter how badly your flesh wants to rise up, hold your tongue. Don't answer back.

LAMENTATIONS 3:26; PROVERBS 17:28;
PSALM 62:5

### ❖ PRAYER ❖

*I marvel at how Jesus didn't answer His accusers, and I thank You for giving me the same grace and wisdom to know when to speak and when to remain silent. Help me remember that Your glory rests upon me when I face persecution for Christ's sake.*

## Don't Be Afraid to Say No

*Y*OU CAN'T JUDGE someone's heart, but you can judge a person's agenda. When people cozy up to you hoping you'll open a door and you don't open it, then those with a selfish agenda will soon turn cold and move on—and not even look back. Often you will discover that the one who was trying so hard to win your favor suddenly disappears when he figures out you aren't going to give him what he wants.

JOHN 7:24; 1 CORINTHIANS 2:15;
2 TIMOTHY 3:1–5

### ✦ PRAYER ✦

*Relationships can be tricky, but You can't be fooled. Please help me discern the agenda of those who only want to use me or take from me. Show me whom I can really trust and whom I should keep at arm's length. Give me wisdom.*

## March 8

### SHAKE IT ALL OFF

SHAKE OFF THE fear. Shake off the weariness. Shake off the worry. Shake off the disappointment. Shake off the discontent. Shake off the discouragement. Shake off the doubts. Shake off the dread. Shake off every negative thought, and come up higher.

Now is the time to hope and trust in your God. Rise up in Christ, set your face like flint, and determine in your heart to do everything you are called to do. It's no accident you are alive in this hour.

EPHESIANS 6:10; EZEKIEL 3:9; JOHN 16:33

### → PRAYER ←

*I choose this day to shake it all off! I will no longer carry what is contrary to Your heart. Give me the strength to shake off the ties that bind and the weights that hinder me as I run this race. Help me stay determined to press into my calling.*

## Gird Up the Loins of Your Mind

**Y**ou can't be intimate with the devil and not get pregnant with sin. So avoid the wiles of the enemy and stand guard against the spirit of seduction that is waiting and watching for an opportune moment when you are vulnerable to strike.

Gird up the loins of your mind. Guard your heart with all diligence because out of it flows the issues of life. Protect your eye gate and your ear gate. Don't even permit the appearance of evil in your life. Be holy even as I am holy.

1 Peter 1:13; Ephesians 6:11; Proverbs 4:23

### → Prayer ←

*Thank You for the warning. I'm girding and guarding! I am pursuing holiness. Show me if there are any open doors to my heart that the enemy can exploit. Lead me not into temptation and deliver me from evil, and I will sing Your praises forever.*

## March 10

### Draw Healthy Lines in Your Life

*B*OUNDARIES ARE VITAL to a balanced life. Establish your boundaries by My leading; use the self-control and wisdom I have given you to maintain them, even in times of transition. When you do, you'll find greater peace in your life. You have to stay flexible, but setting boundaries won't make you rigid if you follow Me. Don't erect walls; draw healthy lines that don't shut people out.

PROVERBS 25:8; GALATIANS 5:22–23;
2 PETER 1:5–7

### → PRAYER ←

*You make everything so simple. Please break it down for me. Show me where to establish stricter boundaries and where to let the boundaries be looser. By all means, lead me by Your Spirit so that I will do the God things and not just the good things.*

## I Am Holding Your Heart

*I* AM HOLDING YOU. I am holding your hand. I am holding your heart. I am holding you up. I won't let you down. Ever. Keep holding on to Me. Don't let go of My heart because I will never let go of yours. Ever. No one can snatch you out of Father's hand. No one can separate you from the love of Christ. Nothing. No one. Just hold on tight. I know some days it feels like I'm far away, but draw near to Me.

JOHN 10:29; ROMANS 8:31–39; JAMES 4:8

### ✦ PRAYER ✦

*I know You have me in Your grip. I will hold on to Your heart with all that is within me. Please strengthen my inner man. Please show me what to let go of that makes me double-minded. Draw me close to You.*

## March 12

### Who Are You Going to Trust?

*A*RE YOU GOING to trust in Me, or are you going to trust in man? There are many benefits to trusting in Me. There are many disappointments in putting the whole of your trust in man. What can man really do for you that I would not do if I thought it was best for your eternal life? What can man give you that I would not give you if I thought it were wise? Trust in Me. Trust completely in Me. Do not lean on the arm of man.

PSALM 118:8; PSALM 103; JEREMIAH 17:5–8

#### ⤍ PRAYER ⤎

*I am going to trust in You with all my heart. I want all Your benefits to manifest in my life. Show me if there are places in my heart where I am not completely abandoned to Your will. Show me how to develop a more intimate trust in You.*

## I Want to Connect With Your Heart

*I* want to connect with your heart at another level—at a higher level. I want to be the object of your attention and affection. Stop looking at and wondering and worrying about what the enemy is doing and saying to you and about you. The enemy is surely moving, but so am I. Look at Me. Look to Me. Look for Me. I will keep you aware of what you need to know about the enemy. I want to connect with your heart at a higher level.

PSALM 42:7; PHILIPPIANS 1:28; HEBREWS 12:2

### → PRAYER ←

*You are the object of my love. Give me an anointing to love You more. You're greater than any enemy who comes to distract me. Help me keep my heart fixed upon You. Show me how to connect with You at a deeper level, and I will heed Your counsel.*

## WILL YOU LAY DOWN YOUR LIFE IN PRAYER?

*J*ESUS EVER LIVES to make intercession for you. Will you ever live to make intercession for others? Will you lay down your life in prayer for a friend? How about someone you don't even know? Will you focus your prayer on the desires of My heart and trust Me to give you the desires of your heart? Will you die to yourself so others may live? Don't answer too quickly. Think on these things.

HEBREWS 7:25; JOHN 15:13; GALATIANS 2:20

### ✦ PRAYER ✦

*You already know the answer to Your questions. I say yes. I say yes to intercession. I say yes to self-sacrifice. Yet I know I only partly understand what that really means. Give me the grace and self-control to follow through on my yes to Your heart.*

## Resist the Spirit of Offense

*J*UST BECAUSE SOMETHING is truly offensive does not mean you need to bite on the bait of offense. The devil will always take every opportunity to whisper vain imaginations in your spiritual ears that tempt you to take offense, resent, grow bitter, and ultimately walk in unforgiveness toward the offender. Don't take the bait. Don't fall for the trap. Resist the spirit of offense. Being offended is a choice. Don't choose offense. Choose love.

Proverbs 19:11; Matthew 18:21–22; Leviticus 19:18

### → Prayer ←

*Help me to not be easily offended. Help me to overlook sins against me and to truly forgive and bless. Help me to avoid this bait of Satan that tries to trap me with bitter poison. I choose this day not to be offended. I choose to love with Your perfect love.*

## March 16

### SOMETIMES REJECTION IS PROTECTION

Sometimes people's rejection is My protection. Don't look at relationships through natural eyes; instead, ask Me for My perspective. I see all things, and I know all things. I know which relationships will propel you forward and which ones will hold you back, which ones will bless your life and which ones will drain your soul. When people reject relationship with you in the short term, consider that it may be what's best for you in the long term.

PROVERBS 13:20; PSALM 41:9; PSALM 17:8

#### ✦ PRAYER ✦

*I want Your protection. You are a friend
who sticks closer than a brother. You are
a friend who stands with me in adversity.
Help me see Your protection in rejection.
Help me trust that You know not only
what but also who is best for my life.*

## I Want to Share With You

*I* want to lead you. I want to guide you. I want to strengthen you. I want to comfort you. I want to give you grace. I want to pour out My wisdom on you. I want to see you formed into Christ's image fully. I want to take you to new places in Me and show you things to come. I want to share My joy and My secrets with you. What do you want?

Proverbs 25:2; Jeremiah 33:3;
2 Corinthians 3:18

### ✦ Prayer ✦

*You are so gracious in asking me what I want. I want Your leading, Your guidance, Your strength, Your comfort, Your revelations, Your grace, Your wisdom, and Your transforming power. I want to know Your heart. Share Your secrets with me.*

## I Have You Tightly in My Grip

*J*AM HOLDING ON to you. Now if you would only hold on to Me, you could go to new depths and new heights in My love. I never relax My hold on you. I have you tightly in My grip. My hand is upon your life. But sometimes you let go and grab hold of the enemy's thoughts toward you instead of My heart for you. Grab hold of Me and don't let go. Don't let your mind stray. I will help you.

HEBREWS 13:5–6; EPHESIANS 3:18–19;
PSALM 89:13–15

### ☙ PRAYER ❧

*I want to experience the length, the depth, the
width, and the height of Your love for me.
Help me to shun the thoughts of the wicked
one that are contrary to Your heart. Give
me the strength to hold on to You when
my mind starts meditating on subtle lies.*

## I Am Wide Open to You

*I*'VE SEEN YOUR heart—your whole heart. All of it. Nothing is hidden from Me. I see your beautiful heart for Me, how you pursue My friendship, and it moves Me. I want you to know My heart the way I know your heart—completely. I will not hold My heart back from you. I have nothing to fear. I am wide open to you. Seek My heart anew and you will see dimensions of Me that will transform you.

HEBREWS 4:13; JAMES 2:23; JEREMIAH 29:13

### ✦ PRAYER ✦

*My heart is for You though my spirit wars against my flesh. I want to know You intimately. I want to know You the way You know me. Help me stay steady on the journey of seeking You. Give me a persevering heart to chase You in all Your beauty.*

*March 20*

## HOW MUCH DO YOU LOVE ME?

*H*OW MUCH DO you love Me? Really love Me? Stop and consider before you answer. Then answer this: how much do you want to love Me? I know your answer is, "With all my soul, all my strength, all my heart, and all my mind." So what's keeping you from that reality? If you love Jesus, you will keep His commandments. They are not burdensome, and there is grace for you to carry them out. It's up to you.

LUKE 10:27; JOHN 14:21; DEUTERONOMY 7:9

### ❖ PRAYER ❖

*He who is forgiven much loves much—and I love you, but I know I don't love you nearly enough. I need and want to love You more because I can't love others well if I don't love You well. Please change my heart. Turn my heart fully toward You. I want to love You more.*

## YOU ARE VICTORIOUS IN CHRIST

*I*KNOW YOU WANT to do things My way, and that blesses My heart—more than you know. I also know there is a very real enemy roaming about like a roaring lion seeking to devour you. I know that even though your spirit and your will want to press into My will, your flesh is weak. I know on some days it feels like there is a lot working against you. There is. But I am for you, and you are victorious in Christ. Keep pressing in, even when you're not perfect.

ROMANS 8:31; ROMANS 8:34; ISAIAH 59:19

### ✦ PRAYER ✦

*Thank You for assuring me the victory in every battle You lead me into. Thank You for protecting me from the evil one when I am not strong enough to wrestle. Help me to keep pressing in, even when I feel weak. Show me how to press past My flesh to victory.*

## JESUS IS EVERYTHING YOU NEED

ESUS IS YOUR Savior. But His job did not end when you received salvation and Father translated you out of the kingdom of darkness and into the kingdom of light. Jesus is your Savior when sickness attacks your body. He carried away your sickness at Calvary. Jesus is your Savior when demons attack your soul. He's given you a sound mind. He's your Savior when lack presents a problem. He supplies all your needs. Jesus is everything you need all the time. He truly is your saving grace.

COLOSSIANS 1:13; ISAIAH 53:4–5; TITUS 2:11–14

### ⟡ PRAYER ⟡

*I declare: Jesus is my healer; Jesus is my deliverer;*
*Jesus is my everything. Thank You, Holy Spirit,*
*for being faithful to reveal new dimensions of*
*Jesus to my heart. Please continue to give me*
*wisdom and revelation in the knowledge of Christ.*

## WHEN CIRCUMSTANCES
## DEFY THE PROMISE

*Y*OU HAVE A free will, but you are truly free only in Father's will. It may seem like a paradox to your soul, but when you submit your soul to Him, when you surrender your heart to Him, when you put your life and everything that concerns you in His hands and trust His direction, then you will have peace even when circumstances defy the truth of the promise. Give up and give yourself completely to your heavenly Father.

ROMANS 12:2; MARK 14:35–36; PROVERBS 23:26

### ✦ PRAYER ✦

*I surrender all. I surrender my life, my thoughts, my words, my everything. Help me truly put all that I have and all that I am in Father's hands. Teach me how to surrender anew if I begin to get selfish. Show me how to walk a life of self-sacrifice unto Father.*

## March 24

### TAKE THE LIMITS OFF

*T*HINK ABOUT WHAT you want out of life. Think about what you want in your family. Think about what you want in your career. Think about what you want in your health. Most importantly, think about what you want in our relationship. Now realize this: I am able to do more than you can ask, think, or imagine. Dream big, take the limits off, and petition heaven. Sometimes you have not because you ask not.

2 TIMOTHY 2:7; PROVERBS 23:7; JAMES 4:3

### ✦ PRAYER ✦

*Help me think strategically. Help me think rightly. Help me think the way You think. Show me where I have limited myself with my own thinking. Teach me how to dream bigger than I've ever dreamed before. Show me Your dreams.*

## Fear Leads You Away From My Heart

*F*EAR WILL LEAD you nowhere good. Fear leads you away from My heart, My promises, My provision, and everything else I am trying to put into your hands. Fear is not just an obstacle to overcome; it's also a spirit that you have to fight just like you would a thief who comes into your home. Fear comes to steal, kill, and destroy—and it will if you let it. Will you let fear wreak havoc on your life, or will you choose to rise up in your authority and in the blessing and choose faith?

John 14:27; Matthew 6:34; Isaiah 43:1

### → Prayer ←

*I refuse to allow fear to wreak havoc on my life. I reject all worry and anxiety. I choose life, peace, and overwhelming joy. Send your angels, who hearken to the voice of Father and His words, to protect me from the assignments of the enemy.*

## YOUR PRAYERS DO NOT
## FALL ON DEAF EARS

*I* WILL NEVER HOLD any good thing back from you. Father takes every petition into consideration as it reaches His throne of grace. Your prayers do not fall on deaf ears. He answers them with His wisdom, in His timing. His wisdom is pure and peaceable. Don't lose heart if you don't see the answers right now. I will never hold any good thing back from you. Trust Me. Trust Jesus. Trust your heavenly Father.

HEBREWS 4:16; PSALM 84:11; JAMES 3:17

### ✦ PRAYER ✦

*I know Father hears me when I pray. I know He answers me when I pray according to His will. Still, sometimes I do not know how to pray as I ought. Would You help me pray perfect prayers? Would You show me Father's plans so I can pray and agree?*

## There Is Always a Reason to Hope

*H*OPE IS SUCH a powerful force. Faith is the substance of things hoped for. Without hope, there is no faith. So hope against hope, as Abraham did according to Romans 4:18. Let hope be the anchor of your soul, stabilizing your emotions during the trials and tribulations that come to discourage your heart. Let hope arise in your emotions. Think hopeful thoughts. No matter what situation you encounter, no matter how hopeless things look, there is always a reason to hope in Christ.

ROMANS 12:12; ROMANS 15:13; PSALM 39:7

### ✦ PRAYER ✦

*I will hope always. All those who hope in the Lord will never be put to shame. Please help me discern the very first signs of any attack against the hope that is within me. Teach me to meditate on Christ in me, the hope of glory. Like Abraham, I will hope against hope.*

*March 28*

## Look to Your Helper

You can choose to be overwhelmed in the face of an overwhelming situation. You can allow "overwhelm" to oppress you, depress you, and convince you to turn your thoughts from Christ. You can choose to let it consume you and confuse you and harass you. Or you can look to your helper. I am your helper. I am always with you. You need not be overwhelmed. I am always standing by to help.

2 Corinthians 12:9; John 8:32; Galatians 5:1

### ✦ Prayer ✦

*I choose not to be overwhelmed. I choose to immediately turn to You for the help You so freely offer to give me. So help me not to come to the edge of "overwhelm." Warn me when I am coming dangerously close to overextending myself or thinking wrong thoughts.*

## I Will Show You as You Go

*I* know you like to have everything figured out ahead of time. I know you like to analyze and plan and prioritize. I know you like to discern the direction and map your steps. But sometimes you don't need to know. Sometimes I lead you on a need-to-know basis. Rest assured that I will show you what you need to see and tell you what you need to hear right in time for you to make the right move. I really will.

2 Samuel 7:28; Psalm 9:10; Psalm 20:7

### ✦ Prayer ✦

*You know me so well. Help me not to get anxious about the days ahead. Show me how to cast off those cares and shut off my mind so I can hear Your still, small voice speaking. Make me content knowing what I need to know in the moment and nothing more.*

## March 30

## A Word About Your Thought Life

*H*ow would your thought patterns change if you exalted Jesus in every area of your life? How would the words of your mouth change if you purposely exalted Jesus with your lips? How would your actions and reactions change if you decided to exalt Jesus through your behavior? What if you lived every part of your life to exalt the King of kings and Lord of lords? How would it change you? I can help you get there if you'll let Me. I want to see Christ exalted.

PSALM 139:2; PSALM 139:23; HEBREWS 3:1

### ✦ PRAYER ✦

*My life would change radically if I rid myself of thoughts that don't belong in my mind and praised Jesus continually with my lips. Teach me how to make the changes I need to make so that Christ is exalted in my life. Help me press past the opposition.*

## STOP BEING SO HARD ON YOURSELF

*Y*OU ARE SO, so hard on yourself sometimes. So hard. Christ is the One who changes you from glory to glory. You can't change yourself. You can study the Scriptures. You can pray. You can cultivate My fruit in your life. You can choose to die daily. But even in all of that, you need My help. Apart from Christ you can do nothing. Stop trying so hard. Lean into My sufficient grace to make the spiritual progress you desire. We're in this together.

2 CORINTHIANS 3:18; JOHN 15:5;
2 CORINTHIANS 12:9

### ✦ PRAYER ✦

*You are so, so gracious. I want to do what's right, and I do take it hard when I fall short. Please help me not to take on guilt and condemnation, especially over issues that are not grieving Your heart. As You lead me into the next glory, help me see how far I've come.*

# April

*It will be, if you will diligently obey My command-
ments which I am commanding you today, to love
the Lord your God, and to serve Him with all your
heart and with all your soul, then I will give you the
rain of your land in its season, the early rain and the
latter rain, that you may gather in your grain and
your wine and your oil. I will provide grass in your
fields for your livestock, that you may eat and be full.*

—Deuteronomy 11:13–15

## My Thoughts Toward You Are Lovely

**M**Y THOUGHTS TOWARD you are true. My thoughts toward you are honest. My thoughts toward you are just. My thoughts toward you are pure. My thoughts toward you are lovely. My thoughts toward you produce a good report about you. Let your thoughts about yourself, your circumstances, your friends and family—and about Me—line up with My thoughts, and you will see breakthroughs on all sides.

PSALM 92:5; AMOS 4:13; 1 CORINTHIANS 2:11

### → PRAYER ←

*Show me Your thoughts. Tell me how You think and feel about me. Reveal Your heart, and I will declare Your thoughts with my mouth. I will meditate on how You see me and reject thoughts that try to paint me in any other light.*

# April 2

## I Want to Tell You My Secrets

*I* WANT TO TAKE you to a new place in Me. I want to show you things to come so you can agree with Me in prayer, thought, and deed. I want to tell you secrets of My heart for your loved ones and give you strategies to make effective intercession for their souls. I want to open up a new realm of spiritual realities that will bless you. I want to do that and so much more. Are you willing to go with Me?

### JOHN 16:13; ROMANS 8:26; LUKE 9:23

### ✦ PRAYER ✦

*Yes, Holy Spirit, I am willing to go with You wherever You want to take me. I know it won't always be comfortable because I will have to die to myself to fully embrace Your best for me. Please give me the grace to keep following You all my days.*

## ASK ME WHAT I THINK

Stop looking at your problems through natural eyes—just for a moment. Meditating on your circumstances can breed fear in your heart and discouragement in your soul. Looking at present realities can paralyze your reasoning and confuse you. Ask Me instead what I think about your current situation. Ask Me for wisdom and guidance and strategies. I have a different perspective than you do. I have all the answers. Ask Me.

Romans 8:28; James 1:5; Isaiah 55:9

### → PRAYER ←

*Holy Spirit, I'm asking You for wisdom. I'm asking You for strategies. I'm asking You for counsel. Help me see Your perspective on my life. Your ways are higher than my ways, and Your thoughts are higher than my thoughts. Show me Your ways.*

## April 4

### I Know Where You Need to Go

ON'T THINK TOO far ahead. It can be overwhelming and confusing and frustrating. I see the end from the beginning. I know where you need to go, what you need to do, and what you don't need to do. I know what you need to say and what you don't need to say. Take things one day at a time and ask Me what to do, where to go, who to talk to, and what to say. I will make it all plain and clear to you as you go. Trust Me.

Isaiah 46:10; Psalm 37:23; Luke 12:12

### → PRAYER ←

*Holy Spirit, help me not to get ahead of myself.*
*Help me not to get ahead of You. Thank You*
*for ordering my steps as I delight myself in You.*
*Thank You for making my paths straight and*
*teaching me the words to say at the right time.*

## You Can Always Count On This

ONE THING YOU can absolutely always count on in life is My love for you. I love with a passion. I love you with all My mind, heart, and strength. I love you with a perfect love that will cast out all fear, rejection, and worry—and anything else that does not belong in your soul. I love you just the way you are, and nothing will ever change that. Nothing. Believe that.

1 John 4:18; Romans 8:38–39; Zephaniah 3:17

### ✦ Prayer ✦

*You are so faithful and true. Your love is purer than gold. Thank You for reassuring my heart that You are with me. I know that You are always near me. Help me to sense Your presence more and more and to share Your heart with others.*

## April 6

## WHEN TO HIT THE RESET BUTTON

Sometimes you just have to hit the reset button. Start over. Reject the thoughts that led you to where you are. Repent. Change the way you think about your life. Every thought you think needs to be taken captive to the lordship of Jesus Christ. Every word you speak should be seasoned with grace and motivated by love. You can decide to walk this way now. I will help you.

ROMANS 8:5–6; PHILIPPIANS 4:8;
COLOSSIANS 4:6

### ✦ PRAYER ✦

*Holy Spirit, help me get my thoughts, my words, and my actions in line with Your heart. Where I am lacking, please pour out Your grace upon me so that I can have the strength to press past what's pressing against me. I want love to motivate me.*

## My Peace Dwells Within You

Maintain your peace. Don't let people steal it. Don't let situations steal it. Don't let your emotions steal it. Don't let the devil steal it. Peace is a priceless commodity, and ultimately it's easier to keep than it is to get back. My peace dwells on the inside of you. Jesus is your Prince of Peace. So hold on to Me, follow Me, and watch Me, and you will stay in perfect peace.

Psalm 29:11; Psalm 37:37; Psalm 119:165

### ✤ Prayer ✤

*You have promised me peace. Since it is coming from the Prince of Peace, I know You will deliver on this promise. Help me do my part. Help me to set my eyes on You. Help me not to look too long at what is going wrong but instead to gaze at the One who is righteous.*

## April 8

### TRUST ME IN THE LIMBO

*L*IVING IN LIMBO is never comfortable. Not knowing what is going to happen next can be a hard thing—unless you trust in Me. I know what is going to happen next, and then after that. I know where I am leading you and what will oppose you and how to overcome it. I know all things, and I am leading you and guiding you into all truth. So trust Me in the limbo. I won't leave you hanging. I won't leave you without help.

1 PETER 5:7; PSALM 55:22; HEBREWS 10:35

### ✦ PRAYER ✦

*You have earned my confidence through Your faithfulness. You have always led me through transitions. When I get to the next uncertain season, help me remember the last time around. Show me how to navigate where I am so I can get where You want me to go.*

## LIFT UP YOUR SHIELD OF FAITH

**D**ON'T LET ANYTHING sway your heart from faith in Father's Word. Don't allow the enemy to use his smoke and mirrors to pull you into fear. Resist the temptation to step onto the road of doubt and unbelief. Lift up the shield of faith now, and it will do what it is supposed to do— it will quench every fiery dart of the enemy. Lift the shield, and lift it high, and know that perfect love casts out fear. Don't let fear torment you anymore.

1 JOHN 5:5; EPHESIANS 6:16; 1 JOHN 4:18

### ✦ PRAYER ✦

*I will walk by faith and not by sight. I will move in faith that overcomes the world. I will stand in faith with nothing wavering. Help me resist the evil one's lies and the fears and doubts he tempts me with. Teach me to guard my heart from faith-stealers.*

## April 10

### RESIST FEELINGS OF DISAPPOINTMENT

DISAPPOINTMENTS WILL ALWAYS come. People—even people you love dearly—will disappoint you. Circumstances and outcomes will disappoint you. You will certainly disappoint yourself at times, and you will even feel during certain seasons that Father has not come through at the right time with the answers to your prayers. Resist disappointment like you would resist the devil because many times it is the voice of the enemy. He is trying to sow seeds of disappointment in your heart.

PHILIPPIANS 4:6–7; ROMANS 8:28; PSALM 42:11

### ✦ PRAYER ✦

*Disappointments have come, but You are always with me to give me a future and a hope. Thank you for always being there to remind me of the Word and shine a light on the truth. Help me resist those feelings of disappointment when they arise.*

## BE AWARE OF MY PRESENCE AT ALL TIMES

*B*EING ALONE IN My presence has great value. Corporate prayer and worship has great value. Gathering together, just two or three, has great value. I am with you wherever you go. I am always there ready to fellowship with you, ready to refresh you, ready to speak to your heart, ready to strengthen you. No matter where you find yourself, look for Me. You'll find Me.

PSALM 16:11; PSALM 27:8; JEREMIAH 29:13

### → PRAYER ←

*I value Your presence more than life itself. In Your presence there is fullness of joy. Help me to discern Your Spirit in my midst. Help me to recognize the reality of Your presence everywhere I am and everywhere I go.*

## April 12

### THINK AND SPEAK THE OPPOSITE

THOUGHTS HAVE ASSIGNMENTS and purpose. The enemy whispers his thoughts into your mind to bring fear, worry, depression, anger, grief, and many other emotions.

You must be purposeful about resisting the temptation to think on the negativity the wicked one suggests. You must reject the thoughts, even if they match your feelings. You must think the opposite and speak the opposite. That's how you cancel the enemy's assignment and thwart his purpose.

2 CORINTHIANS 10:3–6; EPHESIANS 4:22–24;
COLOSSIANS 3:2–5

### → PRAYER ←

*I have never considered thoughts as the enemy's assignments, but certainly they are among his fiery darts. Help me avoid this evil snare. You've given me the Spirit of self-control. Help me exercise control over my thought life.*

## You Can Change Direction

*I*f you don't like the way your life is heading, change direction. If you don't like the circumstances in your life, change your thoughts, words, and deeds, and your course will change. It doesn't always happen overnight. Know this and give Me the time to work with your prayers, but keep thinking good thoughts, proclaiming the Word, and breaking habits and patterns that have led you to the place where you currently find yourself.

Mark 7:20–23; 1 Corinthians 11:1;
1 Thessalonians 5:17

### → Prayer ←

*I love Your practical advice. I have the power
to change what I don't like about my life, and
I am determined to do what it takes to make
those changes. But I need Your all-sufficient grace
to empower me to press through to victory.*

*April 14*

## When You Feel Weak, Lean on Me

*L*ET THE WEAK say, "I am strong." Let the weak say, "With God nothing will be impossible" (Luke 1:37). Let the weak say, "I can do all things through Christ who strengthens me." I know you feel weak sometimes—too weak to take another step, too weak to raise your shield of faith, too weak to pray. When you feel weak, lean on Me. I am your strengthener. I am able to make you stand. I am your intercessor. You can do this.

2 CORINTHIANS 12:10; PSALM 37:39;
PHILIPPIANS 4:13

### ✦ PRAYER ✦

*I am strong! Help me remember You are with me and that Your strength is available to me when I feel weak, when I feel overwhelmed, when I feel like I can't fight another day. Strengthen me in my inner man so I can stand and withstand.*

## LET THIS STRENGTHEN YOUR FAITH

*I* WANT TO REVEAL mysteries to your heart that will strengthen your faith. I want to reveal things about Myself to you that will cause you to trust Me all the more. I want to show you prayer answers that you didn't recognize so you will have more confidence that I am working in your life when you can't see it or feel it. Pray with me. Come away with Me. I am waiting.

1 CORINTHIANS 13; MATTHEW 16:17;
ROMANS 8:26

### ✦ PRAYER ✦

*I want to know everything about You. I
know that the closer I get to You, the more
I see Your beauty in action, and the more
I will want to press into greater revelations
about Your love. Show me everything You
want me to see—and help me see it.*

## RESIST THE ATTACKS

THE DEVIL WANTS to bring disillusionment to your soul. He wants to choke the love out of you with distrust. He wants to discourage you to the point of giving up. He wants to depress you so that you will lie down and not get back up again—so he can kick you while you are down. But I say to you, look at the beauty of Jesus your Savior and consider His love for you. Think about Father's love for you and fight those troubling feelings. Resist the attacks.

MARK 13:22; DANIEL 7:25; ROMANS 5:8

### ⇢ PRAYER ⇠

*I refuse to give place to the enemy in any area*
*of my life. You are able to make me stand,*
*and You have given me your whole armor.*
*Help me to submit myself to You completely*
*and resist the devil so that he will flee.*

## DON'T COMPLICATE THINGS

ON'T MAKE THINGS more complicated than they need to be. You make things complicated by thinking too much about them, which causes you to make assumptions, worry, and strive.

When My grace is on a thing, it's easy. You may still have resistance, but there is grace to press back against the resistance. You may still face challenges, but My grace is sufficient to overcome the challenges on the road to your destiny. Don't overthink it. Just walk with Me.

1 PETER 5:7; PROVERBS 12:25; MATTHEW 6:27

### ✦ PRAYER ✦

*I don't want to worry and fret and allow anxiety to dictate my thoughts. Help me to discern Your grace, tap into Your grace, move out into Your grace, and by all means understand Your grace. Help me to walk with You throughout the day.*

## I Will Manifest Your Healing

I AM THE GOD who heals you. I heal every part of you. I bring healing to your physical body. I bring healing to your soul. I heal every sickness. I heal every disease. I heal every hurt. I heal every wound. I heal every ill and every ailment. Nothing shall by any means harm you. Put all of your trust in Me—all of it. Lean fully on My grace, and I will manifest the healing you need. Assuredly I will.

JEREMIAH 17:14; 1 PETER 2:24; PSALM 103:2–4

### ✦ PRAYER ✦

*I want to walk in divine health. Give me a greater and greater revelation of Your healing power. I want to lay hands on the sick and see them recover. Please give me the boldness to step out in faith and release Your healing anointing.*

## I Will Make My Will Known

Don't allow yourself to get overanxious about finding or missing My will. I assure you that I have ways to get through to you even amid your frustrations and confusion. I am able to lead you and guide you into all truth. You don't need to worry or fear. You don't need to rely on your own reasoning to figure things out. Just keep walking with Me and have confidence that I am ordering your steps, because I am.

PHILIPPIANS 2:13; PSALM 138:8; PSALM 40:8

### → PRAYER ←

*I long to know Your good, perfect, and acceptable will for my life. But I will trust You to lead me and guide me even when I cannot hear You clearly, even when You choose not to share with me exactly where I am headed. Help me to totally surrender to You.*

*April 20*

## EMBRACE THE REFINER'S FIRE

Many people want My winds to blow in their lives. Many want Me to rain down on their lives. But fewer want the refiner's fire that will purify their hearts and remove things that hinder spiritual growth. Fewer want the refiner's fire because it is uncomfortable. Yes, sometimes it burns, but it only burns away those unnecessary, unprofitable things that hinder love. Will you embrace the refiner's fire?

ZECHARIAH 13:9; 1 PETER 1:7; ISAIAH 48:10

### → PRAYER ←

*I want the refiner's fire. I want You to purify my heart. I want You to remove anything that hinders my walk with You. I give You permission to do what it takes to bring my poor qualities to the surface so I can repent of them and walk in freedom.*

## Go Ahead and Rejoice Now

*I*F YOU COULD see the end from the beginning as I do, you'd let go of the reasoning, imaginations, worries, fears, and discouragement that try to plague you. If you could see the end from the beginning, you would rejoice, and rejoice again. Trust Me. I see the end from the beginning, and all things really are working together for your good. Believe Me, and go ahead and rejoice now. What are you waiting for?

PSALM 118:24; PSALM 5:11; PSALM 150

### ✦ PRAYER ✦

*Show me things to come. Show me the path*
*ahead, or just show me another glimpse of*
*Your faithfulness, and I will rejoice. Help me*
*to remember to rejoice in the storms. Move*
*upon my heart to remember that the end*
*is triumphant and eternal in Christ.*

## April 22

### I Am Unshakable

*I* NEVER CHANGE. I am constant. I am consistent. I am steadfast. I will not act one way toward you today and another way toward you tomorrow. My love for you is solid. I am unmovable. I am unshakable. There's nothing you can do to surprise Me. I love you when you miss the mark. I am not going anywhere. I am always here for you under any and every circumstance. I never change.

MALACHI 3:6; HEBREWS 13:8; HEBREWS 13:5

### ✦ PRAYER ✦

*I am glad You never change, but I need to change. Help me to move from faith to faith and from glory to glory. Help me not to be surprised when I fall short of Your glory. Give me greater confidence in Your promise to always stand with me.*

## I Will Meet You in Your Praise

*I* AM LOOKING FOR worshippers. I am
looking for those who will praise the name
of Jesus. I am looking for those who adore the King
and are willing to express His majesty. I am looking
for those who will worship Father in spirit and in
truth.

I love to dwell in your praise and worship. I love
to manifest My presence, My gifts, My wisdom, My
counsel, and everything that I am in your adoration.
I love to show up in the high praises, in the shouting
and dancing, in the tears of joy, and in the stillness
of your soul. I am looking for worshippers to dwell
with. What do you say?

JOHN 4:24; ISAIAH 12:5; HEBREWS 13:15

### ✦ PRAYER ✦

*You have found a worshipper in me. Help
me find that place in praise where nothing
else matters but rejoicing in Your love. Take
me to deeper places in worship where I
can dwell with You, hear Your voice, see
Your beauty, and enjoy Your presence.*

## April 24

### I Am Eagerly Waiting on You

*I* AM LISTENING. I am always listening. All it takes for you to get My attention is to turn your heart in My direction. Just a whisper causes Me to bow My ear down to you. My eyes are always upon you. I am watching over you carefully. I am always with you everywhere you go. I'm just waiting—eagerly waiting—for you to start the conversation. So let's talk. I have wisdom waiting for you. Speak to me, and I will speak to you.

PSALM 31:2; PSALM 86:1; PSALM 121:5

### ◈ PRAYER ◈

*You are amazing. You always hear my cries. You make intercession for me to Father, praying perfect prayers according to His will. Inspire my heart to run after You and find You where you are waiting. I am listening.*

## TURN TO ME FIRST

Sometimes when you are going through troubles and trials, you turn to everyone but Me. I don't understand why you don't come to Me first. I watch you struggle against the accusations the enemy throws at your mind, those flaming missiles of hate. I hear you cry out to your friends for counsel. That's fine, but know and remember that I am your Counselor. Turn to Me first.

PSALM 55:22; PSALM 119:105; PSALM 18:6

### ✦ PRAYER ✦

*I don't understand why I don't come to You first either. You are my Counselor, my Helper, my Comforter. Help me remember to run to You when the trials, troubles, and temptations come. Interrupt my thoughts with Your loving voice.*

## April 26

## I Am Helping You Reach Your Destiny

Have confidence in Me. Have faith in Me. Have trust in Me. Know that I have your back. I am your rear guard. Put your hope in Me. Expect Me to protect you. Keep your eyes on Me. Set your thoughts on Me. If you do these things, you will completely slam the door on voices that are contrary to Father's plan for your life. I am helping you reach your destiny. Listen to Me.

Psalm 138:8; Isaiah 52:12; Isaiah 46:10

### → Prayer ←

*You go before me to make a way for me. You are behind me to watch my back. You are everywhere all the time, and I am thankful. Help me to sense Your presence as I walk through each day. Help me stay on the path toward my destiny.*

## High Praise Brings Victory

*Y*our praise really is a weapon of warfare. Your weapons of warfare are not carnal, but mighty through Father to pull down strongholds. High praise will pull down those lofty imaginations that batter your mind. High praise is like a battering ram in the spirit. Father inhabits the praises of His people—and so do I. Release your high praise, and you will see the enemy flee from attacking your mind.

Psalm 71:8; Psalm 69:30; Isaiah 25:1

### → Prayer ←

*I am your battle-ax, and I will praise You! I give You thanks for the victory! I praise You for Your righteous acts and Your saving grace. I shout for joy to the King of all the earth and glorify the name of the Lord. Your praise will ever be on my lips.*

## April 28

### GIVE ME YOUR DREAMS AND AMBITIONS

*A*LL I REALLY want from you is you. If you give Me all that you are, if you give Me your dreams and ambitions, if you give Me your love and adoration, if you give Me your faith and trust, if you give Me all of you, then I can radically change your life, and your circumstances will not move you. I will change you into the image of Christ, and everything else will fall into place.

PSALM 37:4; MATTHEW 6:21; PROVERBS 13:12

### ☙ PRAYER ❧

*I surrender all—and those are not just mere words. I'm willing to lay it all down for You like Christ laid it all down for me. I am willing to give You everything I have. Help me keep seeking the kingdom of God above all else so that all the other things Father has promised will be added to me.*

## FATHER IS IN CONTROL

**W**HAT DO YOU think would happen if you were to let go and let Me? What if you were to let go of your preconceived notions of how life should be and let Me show you a better life? What if you were to let go of your ideas and plans for the future and let Me show you My ideas and plans for the future? Stop trying to figure out everything, and don't worry if things don't line up the way you think they should. Father is in control.

PSALM 37:5; PROVERBS 16:3: PROVERBS 16:9

### ✦ PRAYER ✦

*What do I think would happen if I gave You control? I imagine I would find more peace, rest, and joy. I imagine I would have more faith and trust in You. I imagine I would rest and relax more easily. I see Your point. Help me let go and let You do what You do best. I give you the reins.*

*April 30*

## YOU MOVE MY HEART

Your selflessness moves My heart. It strikes Me how you set your own needs aside to help others at your own expense. You've grown. There was a time when you looked out for yourself and only yourself. The love of God is working through you as you extend a helping hand even when it's not convenient. Father's love has truly been shed abroad in your heart, and it's a beautiful sight.

PHILIPPIANS 2:4; 1 PETER 3:8;
1 THESSALONIANS 5:15

### → PRAYER ←

*I'm glad You noticed. Thank You for the affirming words. I treasure them. Please continue to shed Your love abroad in my heart so that I can give from a well that never runs dry. Help me identify the needs in the lives of those around me so I can show them what Your love looks like.*

# May

*For if I pray in an unknown tongue, my spirit
prays, but my understanding is unfruitful. What
is it then? I will pray with the spirit, and I will
pray with the understanding. I will sing with the
spirit, and I will sing with the understanding.*

—1 Corinthians 14:14–15

## Be an Agent of Blessing

B LESS EVERYONE YOU come in contact with. Bless them with your words. Bless them with your kindness. Bless them with a smile in passing. Bless them with your thoughts and your deeds. Too many people in the world today have nothing good to say. Too many people speak ill of one another. Too many people break their word. You set the example. Bless, and curse not. Bless, bless, and continue blessing.

LUKE 6:38; ISAIAH 1:19; EPHESIANS 1:3

### ✦ PRAYER ✦

*I will bless the Lord at all times—and I will bless Your people. I will bless those who curse me. I will bless those who bless me. I will bless those who hurt me. I will bless those who help me. Teach me how to be a blessing to everyone around me everywhere I go. I know that blesses You.*

## May 2

## I HAVE MARKED YOU FOR VICTORY

*I* HAVE MARKED YOU for victory. I have marked you for destiny. I have marked you for love. See yourself the way that I see you. Embrace the reality that you are more than a conqueror in Christ. Relish the understanding that greater is He who is in you than he who is in the world. Choose by your will to believe what the Word says about you over what the enemy, people, or your own thoughts insist. You are a new creation. Walk worthy of your calling.

DEUTERONOMY 20:4; PSALM 108:13;
1 CORINTHIANS 15:57

### → PRAYER ←

*How can I lose? You live on the inside of me. You are directing me, giving me wisdom, and showing me things to come. Teach me to see myself victorious in every situation. Show me how to shift my mind quickly from thoughts of discouragement and defeat to thoughts of victory and triumph.*

## ASK FATHER FOR RESTORATION

*P*EOPLE TELL YOU that the devil does not fight fair. That's true, of course. He's a liar, a thief, a destroyer, and a killer. But always remember this: you have the advantage over the wicked one because I am on your side. I never lose a battle. I can restore and redeem and reconcile the things and people your adversary has tried to kill, steal, and destroy. Ask Father for restoration.

JOHN 10:10; ROMANS 8:31; JOEL 2:25

### ⁂ PRAYER ⁂

*You are a victorious God, and I have the ultimate victory in You. Please restore to me what the enemy has stolen, murdered, or otherwise destroyed. Show me how to regain what was lost. Help me to battle until I see the spoils of war.*

*May 4*

## Keep Forging Ahead Even Without the Why

W━━HEN I LEAD you and guide you to go somewhere or to do something, you may not know up front why I have given you the assignment. You may move forward in faith and run into obstacles and circumstances you did not expect. They may not be pleasant. Don't quit. Don't pull back. Don't let that frustrate you. Remember that I have sent you to that person or to that place, and receive My grace to press past the obstacles. Look for My hand in the matter but be ready to continue forging ahead even if you don't understand the why.

2 Corinthians 12:8–10; Matthew 17:20; John 16:33

### → Prayer ←

*I expect there to be obstacles in my path because the enemy is not going to lie down and let me take ground for Your kingdom. Help me keep my eyes on the prize. Help me keep going with blind trust even when I can't hear Your still, small voice. Give me courage to press on.*

## COMPLAINING WON'T CHANGE A THING

*Y*ou should know this by now, but I will tell you again: complaining won't do you any good. Complaining won't change anything. Complaining does not change the spiritual climate over your life. In fact, it makes it worse. Turn your groaning into praising. Turn your grumbling into thanksgiving. Turn your griping into worship. As you do, you will shift your mind and heart toward answers to the issues you are complaining about.

PHILIPPIANS 2:14; EPHESIANS 4:29; JAMES 5:9

### ✦ PRAYER ✦

*I know it does me no good to complain. It only makes me miserable, yet I moan and groan more than I'd like to admit. Help me to keep Your praise on my lips. Show me the things that are praiseworthy and help me set my mind on excellent things that evoke worship in my heart.*

## May 6

### DON'T WORRY ABOUT YOUR PROVISION

*W*HEN THE ENEMY messes with your finances, it can strike fear in your soul. When you take that financial hit, it can bring worry and doubt and a flood of other emotions to your mind. Remember, the lilies do not toil nor do they spin, yet they are clothed. The birds do not sow or reap or store food, but they are fed. Don't worry about what you will eat or drink or what clothes you put on. Father will not leave you without the things you need. He will not.

2 CORINTHIANS 9:8; PSALM 37:25–26;
PHILIPPIANS 4:11–15

#### → PRAYER ←

*I love it when You speak the Word to me.*
*Thanks for reminding me of Father's promises*
*to supply all my needs. When the enemy tries*
*to bring fear of lack to my soul, quicken my*
*tongue to speak these promises out of my mouth*
*boldly and with confidence in Your love.*

## I Will Give You the Desires of Your Heart

*T*HE ANSWER TO your problem is in Me. The provision for your needs is in Me. The wisdom that you are after is in Me. Everything your heart ultimately desires and all of your hopes and dreams are in Me. So seek Me. Chase after Me. Pursue Me at a new level. Draw close to Me, and I will draw close to you. Look for Me day and night. Talk with Me. Walk with Me. Delight yourself in Me, and I will give you the desires of your heart.

1 Chronicles 16:11; Lamentations 3:25; Isaiah 55:6–7

### → Prayer ←

*You are my everything and have everything I need—and everything I want. Show me what to set aside so I can spend more time with You. Thwart the enemy's plans to steal my time and distract me from Your heart. Show me how to diligently pursue You and delight myself in You.*

## May 8

### Choose to Believe the Best About Your Heavenly Father

Some clichés are clichés for a good reason. There is a large measure of truth in many of them. "It's darkest before the dawn." Father is not usually early, but He's never late. He's always right on time. "There's a blessing in the storm." These may sound like pat answers when you are walking through the fire, but they can be hopeful statements if you allow them to be. Choose to believe the best about your heavenly Father. He believes the best about you.

Psalm 27:14; Ecclesiastes 8:6;
Lamentations 3:22–23

### ✦ Prayer ✦

*When You put it that way, I realized I need to repent. I don't always believe the best about You. Help me to cast down the arguments the devil raises about You. Help me see You as You really are, in all of Your mercy and justice. Help me remain steadfast in Your perfect love.*

## WHAT'S YOUR SPIRITUAL TEMPERATURE?

**W**HAT'S YOUR SPIRITUAL temperature? I'm not asking because I don't know. I know all things. I am asking because I want you to assess your heart. Are you satisfied with your level of passion for Jesus? Are you content with the fervor of your prayer life? Are you burning hot enough? Are you shining brightly enough? I am not asking you to make you feel bad. I'm inviting you to come closer to Me. If you want to raise your spiritual temperature, just come closer to Me.

JAMES 4:8; HEBREWS 11:6; HEBREWS 10:22

### ✦ PRAYER ✦

*As always, You're asking a question that causes me to examine my heart, and I don't want to answer too quickly. Help me see what You see. Help me understand what keeps me from coming closer to You. Draw me into Your presence. Give me a hunger I cannot deny.*

## May 10

### DON'T LOOK AT THE IMPOSSIBILITIES

*Y*OU KNOW THAT I will never ask you to do something impossible. It may look impossible; it may sound impossible; it may feel impossible. But remember this: nothing is impossible to the one who believes. So believe when I give you an instruction that I will grace you, strengthen you, and help you in every way to obey the command. Believe there is a strength to endure the rough terrain on the journey. Believe there is a reward waiting for you. Stay focused on the promise, and it will carry you through.

MATTHEW 19:26; LUKE 1:37; JEREMIAH 32:17

### ✦ PRAYER ✦

*You are just, and Your Word is pure. Sometimes what You ask me to do stretches me beyond what I think I can bear, but You know better. Help my unbelief. Help me reject the doubt that clouds my faith. Teach me how to stay my mind on the finish line so I can win my crown.*

## DISCOVER MORE PEACE
## AND JOY ON THIS PATH

*W*HEN YOU TRY to do things in your own strength, you wind up overwhelmed, frustrated, and worn out. I am here to help you. I am here to empower you. I am here to strengthen you. I am here to counsel you. I am here to pray for you and with you. Lean on Me. Rely on Me. Things will work out a lot smoother, a lot cleaner, and a lot easier if you lean and depend on Me and not on your own strength—or your own understanding. Give it a try. You'll discover more peace and joy on this path, I assure you. You'll find everything you need along the way in Me.

ZECHARIAH 4:6; PHILIPPIANS 4:13; PROVERBS 3:5

### ⋅ PRAYER ⋅

*"Overwhelm" is an enemy of my soul. Help me
learn to resist it at the onset. Help me learn
to recognize it and reject it. Help me tap into
the grace that dwells on the inside of me and
apply it to my soul. I want to see my life roll
out according to Your plans and purposes.*

## May 12

### I Am Not Angry When You Stumble

*I* AM NOT DISAPPOINTED in you when you fall. I am not angry with you when you stumble. I am not shocked when you miss the mark. I know the end from the beginning. All of your days are written in a book. I do not rejoice when you fall, stumble, or miss the mark, and it does not take Me by surprise; it does not cause Me to stop loving you; it does not change Father's plans for you. So stop being disappointed in yourself when you fall, angry with yourself when you stumble, and shocked when you miss the mark. Just repent and keep going.

HEBREWS 4:16; 1 JOHN 1:9; PSALM 86:5

### ❖ PRAYER ❖

*I'm so grateful for Your long-suffering and mercy. Your mercies are new every day. Help me embrace this truth in order to combat the guilt and shame that attack my mind when I miss the mark. Teach me how to receive Your forgiveness and continue on my journey.*

## REMEMBER THIS ABOUT ME

*W*HEN YOU DISCOVER My nature—truly discover My nature—you will stop wondering what will happen next. You will stop worrying about things to come. You will stop searching for wisdom from other sources. My nature is love. I am your helper. I am your advocate. I am your standby. I am your intercessor. I am your wisdom, strength, shield, and more. My nature is kind, gentle, long-suffering, and peaceful. Know this about Me now—really know it—and you will remember it later when the trials and storms of life tempt you to question who I am for you.

DEUTERONOMY 32:4; NUMBERS 23:19;
EXODUS 34:6

### ⇢ PRAYER ⇠

*Reveal yourself to me, Holy Spirit. Show me
Your heart in a way I have not yet experienced.
I don't want wisdom that comes from this world.
I want the pure, peaceable, and gentle wisdom
that comes from You. Root me and ground me in
You so I can stand and withstand in the evil day.*

## May 14

### KEEP THE PAST IN THE PAST

*E*VERYONE HAS BAD days. Everyone has down days. Everyone has days they wish they could forget. But I tell you: forget them. Press past those things that are behind. Stop dwelling on the troubles of your past, and stop worrying about the troubles of your future. Press past the mind traffic and focus on Jesus. He left you His peace, peace that passes all understanding, to guard your heart and your mind. So even when you feel discouraged, even when you are anxious, you can tap into that peace that dwells in your spirit. You can press into My heart and find refreshing and strength.

ISAIAH 43:18–19; PHILIPPIANS 3:12–14;
PROVERBS 4:25–27

### ✦ PRAYER ✦

*The past is in the past, yet I am tempted many times to pull it up and rehash it. Help me cast down those thoughts and accept the peace Jesus offers. Help me to resist discouragement and submit myself to Your Word at all times. Show me the way to a deeper relationship with You.*

## SHIFT YOUR THINKING

*A*LL OF THESE things that trouble you—and even the things that delight you—are so temporary. They will all fade away—all of the annoyances, trials, and persecutions. None of this lasts. None of it is eternal. None of it matters beyond this life on Earth. Write eternity on your heart. Consider the eternal impact of your prayers and your works. Shift your thinking.

2 PETER 3:11; 1 TIMOTHY 4:8; JAMES 5:16

### ⟡ PRAYER ⟡

*I live to worship You. Help me worship You all the more. I will sing Your praises all the days of my life. I expect to meet You in that place of praise and worship. Help me shut off the distractions that keep me from entering that heavenly place.*

## May 16

### YOU ARE QUALIFIED IN CHRIST

*T*HE ENEMY TRIES to make you think there's something wrong with you, that you aren't qualified, that you aren't adequate, that you don't have enough experience. The enemy plays with your emotions. He launches oppressive, fiery darts at your soul, imaginations that work against your joy and drive fear into your heart. The truth is, there's nothing wrong with you. You are qualified, adequate, and prepared in Christ for every good work Father calls you to. Don't give thought to the emotional terrorism that's been committed against you. You have My joy and My peace. Believe that.

1 PETER 2:9; EPHESIANS 2:10; ROMANS 8:1

### ⇥ PRAYER ⇤

*I know who I am in Christ—and I need to know it all the more. Open the eyes of my heart and show me who I am in Christ and who He is in me. I am blameless in Father's sight. He delights in me. You delight in me. I know this is true, but I want to experience this truth day in and day out.*

## YOUR RELATIONAL METTLE WILL BE TESTED

**T**HE METTLE OF your relationships will always be tested. The enemy will always come to try to steal, kill, and destroy the covenant relationships Father has appointed and anointed. You can count on this. You have to decide in your heart ahead of time to fight, to war, to stand and withstand the attacks against every divine connection Father brings in your path. On the other hand, not every relationship is meant to be. Some last for a season; others are false and actually open the door to warfare in your life. Ask Me to help you discern the relationships worth fighting for and the ones you need to let go.

PROVERBS 18:24; PROVERBS 27:9;
1 CORINTHIANS 15:33

### ✦ PRAYER ✦

*Lord, help me discern between covenant relationships and those in which people just want to use or abuse me. Show me who I should align with in every season. Help me to be a good friend to others. Give me greater discernment in all my relationships so I can walk according to Your will.*

## May 18

### I Am Always Here for You

*E*VERY SINGLE EFFORT you make to move toward My heart blesses Me. Every time you decide to get up a little earlier to fellowship with Me, pray with Me, or talk with Me, it brings Me joy. I am committed to meeting you in that place, speaking to your heart, refreshing your soul, strengthening your spirit, sharing My wisdom, and just fellowshipping with you. Even when you set aside a few seconds to acknowledge Me, it moves Me. I am committed to your safety and well-being. I am committed to your success. I am always here for you in every situation. And I'm inviting you to lean into Me more and still more.

DEUTERONOMY 7:9; MATTHEW 28:20;
PSALM 33:4

### ✦ PRAYER ✦

*Thank You that You will never leave or forsake me. Thank You that You are as close to me as I want You to be. Show me where I can make more time in my schedule to spend with You. Show me where the little foxes are that spoil the vine of intimacy with You.*

## Let Me Show You When to Say No

*D*on't overcommit yourself. I love that
you let your yes be yes and your no be no. I
love that you are a person of integrity who swears
to your own hurt and does not change your mind.
I love that you are not willing to compromise your
word or your character by shrinking back from a
commitment. Those are admirable character traits
many people lack. But don't overcommit yourself.
Let me show you what to say yes to and what to say
no to. People will pull, tug, and even manipulate.
But I have your best interest at heart. I see the big
picture. I know what's around the corner. So ask
Me and wait for My yes or no.

Proverbs 16:3; Matthew 5:37; Psalm 119:105

### ⇢ Prayer ⇠

*I need Your help. I say yes when I should say
no, when I am already stretched too thin. Help
me to avoid overcommitting myself so that I
don't wear myself out or burn myself out. Give
me the grace to do what You've called me to
do and the wisdom to know what not to do.*

## May 20

### Take Risks That Seem Unusual

*A*NYTHING IS POSSIBLE. All things are possible. Nothing is impossible. Act like you believe those words, for they are true. Take risks that seem unusual. Stretch beyond the limitations of your mind and dream big, pray in faith, intercede with confidence, and stretch out your hands and ask for the healing anointing to flow. All things are possible to the one who believes. I have put My gifts within you. The Spirit who raised Christ from the dead dwells on the inside of you. I am praying with you. You cannot fail if you follow My lead. So listen to My voice, believe I am speaking, step out in faith, take a risk—and watch miracles happen.

MATTHEW 21:22; ROMANS 8:11; LUKE 1:37

### ⤳ PRAYER ⤳

*You know I'm risk averse, but You've given me a measure of faith, and I am willing to exercise the faith You've given me and step out. Help me stay steady and resist any whispers of fear that would try to convince me not to follow Your promptings. Give me boldness.*

## NOTHING BY ANY MEANS
## SHALL HARM YOU

ESUS GAVE YOU power over all the power of the enemy, and nothing by any means shall harm you. Jesus has redeemed you from the curse of the Law, being made a curse for you. For it is written, "Cursed is everyone who hangs on a tree" (Gal. 3:13). You are blessed with every spiritual blessing in heavenly places and are a partaker of Christ's divine nature. You are seated with Him right now. Understand this and operate in this reality. Take authority over the demons that have conspired against your life, and walk in the blessings Father has designated in your life. Model the way of victory for others who are watching.

LUKE 10:19; EPHESIANS 1:3; 2 PETER 1:4

### → PRAYER ←

*Thank You for reminding me of who I really am. I am blessed because Christ has blessed me. Give me a greater and greater revelation of this truth so that I will gain the confidence to rise up and command every force opposing Christ's will in the earth to bow in His name.*

# May 22

## I Will Not Lead You Into Burnout

*P*EOPLE SPEAK TO you about burnout. They tell you that you will grow weary in your race if you run too fast, too hard, too long, or too much. But I say to you that when you follow My leading, when you tap into My grace, when you operate in the anointing that abides, you will not burn out. Jesus's yoke is easy, and His burden is light. When you take on the assignments He gives you, you will not burn out, grow weary, or wear out. You will not. The key to avoiding burnout is simple: follow My leading, listen for My yes and no, and obey what I tell you and show you.

2 Corinthians 12:9; 1 John 2:27; Isaiah 1:19

### ⟶ Prayer ⟵

*I agree with Your words. I break and bind all the words and thoughts of burnout and commit to following Your leading on when to stop and when to go. Help me discern Your will with every invitation, every request, and every demand. Help me know Your will.*

## Remember This When You Are Weary

Wʜᴇɴ ʏᴏᴜ ꜰᴇᴇʟ like you can't take another step, remember that the just shall live by faith and not by feelings. When you feel like nobody is on your side, remember that all of heaven is backing you. When you feel like giving up, remember that Christ prepared good works for you to accomplish before the foundation of the earth. His grace is sufficient for every task He has called you to complete. When you feel overwhelmed by trials and tribulations, remember that Jesus overcame the world. Rejoice in who He is and who you are in Him. Give thanks in everything, pray at all times, and rejoice always.

Rᴏᴍᴀɴs 1:17; Hᴇʙʀᴇᴡs 1:14; 1 Pᴇᴛᴇʀ 4:12

### ✦ Prayer ✦

*Sometimes life just wears me out. I am so grateful You see my weariness and offer refreshing for my body and soul. Help me recognize my own limits. Help me not to let my zeal to do good works override Your wisdom for my life. I will rejoice in You always.*

## May 24

### WILL YOU GIVE UP CHILDISH THINGS FOR MORE OF ME?

What would you do if I told you that I wanted to take you to a place that precious few people will go? What would you do if I extended an invitation to you to explore a place in Me that many will not press into? Would you say yes to My heart? Would you give up the childish things—the things that are not eternally profitable—to follow Me where I would lead you? Would you crucify your flesh and cooperate with Me as we go on a journey together? Would you commit to press past the pain of change, and even chastening, to find new levels of freedom in Christ? I am inviting you. What do you say?

1 CORINTHIANS 13:11; 1 CORINTHIANS 10:23;
GALATIANS 5:24

### → PRAYER ←

*I accept Your invitation with joy and excitement.*
*I say yes to Your heart. I am willing and*
*ready to give up anything that keeps me off*
*Your perfect path for me. Help me walk out*
*my commitment to going on this journey with*
*You. Pour out Your grace and strength.*

## STOP LOOKING AT WHAT WENT WRONG

WHEN THINGS DON'T seem to go your way, look the other way. In other words, when your day doesn't go the way you planned it, when you run into unforeseen problems that derail your agenda, and when you experience setbacks that truly set you back, stop looking at what went wrong. Start looking at what is right. Start looking at Me. Start listening for My voice. Start expecting Me to show you a way over, around, or through. Everything is not going to go your way all the time. You know that. But you can react to this from a place of peaceful assurance—or you can react out of a place of dismay. It depends on where you put your focus. Focus on Me.

PSALM 27:4; JOHN 10:27; ISAIAH 26:3

### ⇥ PRAYER ⇤

*When things don't go my way, I still trust that Jesus is the Way, the Truth, and the Life. Please remind me not to focus on what went wrong but on the One who is right—the One who is righteous. Help me focus on You even when everything around me is trying to distract my heart.*

## May 26

### Keep Asking, and Be Encouraged

Sometimes you have to ask more than once. Sometimes you have to ask more than twice. Sometimes you have to ask over and over. Sometimes you have to ask and keep on asking. You have to knock and keep on knocking. You have to wait and keep on waiting. But when you ask, no matter how many times you ask, ask in faith. Knock with expectance. Wait with excitement. When you ask anything according to the Word, Father hears you. And you know that, if He hears you, He will answer you. The answer may not come right away, but it will come. So keep asking and be encouraged; Father is listening. Your petitions are not falling on deaf ears.

Matthew 7:7; Luke 18:1–8; 1 John 5:15

### ✦ Prayer ✦

*Give me the determination of the persistent widow in Luke 18 who wearied the judge until he heard her cries and answered her plea. Help me to stay steadfast in my faith while I wait for the answer to manifest. Help me endure the waiting period with joy because I know Father hears me.*

## Choose Adoration
## Over Aggravation

Aggravation will get you nowhere. Adoration will take you places in Me that will refresh your soul, give you a new perspective, and strengthen your heart for the day ahead. Why not let go of the aggravations and frustrations that weigh you down? Why not lay aside those weights so that you don't step into besetting sins? Why not meditate on the Word and fellowship with Me instead of meditating on the negative thoughts the enemy is planting in your soul? Why not decide to draw a line in the spiritual sand and think on things that are good, true, and lovely? You'll be much more content if you choose this better path.

Hebrews 1:3; Revelation 5:13; Matthew 22:37

### ⇢ Prayer ⇠

*Help me trade aggravation for adoration.*
*Help me make this divine exchange so that*
*I can receive Your refreshing in the middle*
*of a frustrating day. Help me resist the*
*temptation to be irritated by the annoying*
*circumstances that bog me down.*

## May 28

### You Will Move Toward What You Focus On

*H*ERE IS A life lesson you need to remember: you will always move toward what you focus on. You will always gravitate toward what you look at. If you look at all the things about your friends and family that bother you, they will bother you even more. You'll grow to resent the ones you love. If you look at the things that you appreciate about your friends and family, you'll appreciate those loved ones even more. You'll grow to love the ones you love even more. What you focus on grows, so choose wisely what you focus on. Focus on the good. Love suffers long, is kind, and covers a multitude of sins. Focus on love.

Colossians 3:2; Proverbs 4:25; Matthew 6:33

### ⤞ PRAYER ⤝

*I don't want to make a mountain out of a molehill, but when I meditate on what bothers me, I give it the power to sour my soul. Help me to grow in love for You, for myself, and for the people around me. Help me to focus on what You are doing in my life above all things.*

## WAIT WITH A GOOD ATTITUDE

*N*OBODY LIKES TO sit in a waiting room, even if you are waiting on something good. But much of life is about waiting. Your faith alone is not always enough to immediately manifest Father's will in your life. You see, it's faith mixed with patience that positions you to inherit His yes-and-amen promises. And how you wait is important. When you wait without patience, you delay your own answer. Father is more interested in seeing the character of Christ formed in you than seeing you get immediate answers to every prayer you lift up to the throne. So wait with patience. Wait with endurance. Wait with perseverance. Wait with a good attitude.

LAMENTATIONS 3:25; HABAKKUK 2:3; PSALM 37:7

### ⟿ PRAYER ⟿

*You're so right. I don't like waiting. I'm not the most patient person in the world. Help me wait with a right spirit. Help me wait with a good attitude. Help me wait as if I believe that Your Spirit will break in at any minute and bring the breakthrough I'm hoping to see.*

## May 30

### The Fruit of Obedience

MANY TIMES WHAT you are seeing manifest in your life right now has nothing to do with what you are doing right now. You may be reaping a harvest from seeds you planted in the last season. They might have been good or bad seeds. So don't get discouraged if you are doing the right thing though the wrong thing is happening to you. Keep doing what's right. And don't think that sowing bad seeds today won't bring unwanted consequences tomorrow. The reality, spiritual or natural, is that you reap what you sow. You can repent and receive forgiveness, but sometimes consequences from your actions play out. Live with a healthy fear of the Lord and you will enjoy the fruit of obedience.

John 14:15; Psalm 119:30; 1 John 3:24

### ⇢ Prayer ⇠

*I understand there is seed time and harvest time in my life. I understand I have no power over the time of harvest but that I can keep sowing good seeds even when I am not seeing any fruit from them. Help me to continue sowing, sowing, and sowing in obedience with faith that believes the harvest is coming.*

## GIVE YOURSELF TO THE WORD

GIVE YOURSELF TO the Word, and I will give you the revelation that you desire. For it is I who placed the desire in your heart, and it is My own desire to fulfill it. Yet without your involvement—without your cooperation—I will do nothing. Your part is to abide in the Word, to give yourself over to obedience to Christ's commands, to meditate on the Word day and night—and all throughout the day. I desire to share fuller revelation with you about many things. Will you partner with My heart to press into Jesus?

JOSHUA 1:8; MATTHEW 4:4; JOHN 15:7

### → PRAYER ←

*You're so good to me. Your plans for me are good. Help me do my part. Help me cooperate with Your grace. Show me what I need to do in order to walk in Your perfect will. Tell me how to get to that place of fuller revelation. I am willing to partner with You in any venture You have in mind.*

# June

*You will make known to me the path of life;*
*in Your presence is fullness of joy; at Your*
*right hand there are pleasures forevermore.*

—Psalm 16:11

## YOU ARE HEALED AND WHOLE

*Y*OU ARE HEALED and whole. Walk in it. It is a deception for you to think that you are anything but complete in Christ. It is a lie from the wicked one to keep you pressed down, oppressed and distressed, and even depressed about your past. Forget about past sins. Continue studying My Word about the blood of Jesus and My love for you, and nothing shall stop you. Remember that, because the devil will try to convince you otherwise.

COLOSSIANS 2:10; EPHESIANS 1:7; ROMANS 8:1

### ✦ PRAYER ✦

*I choose this day to walk in the reality that I am fully healed and whole in Christ. The enemy likes to tell me what is wrong with me, but You have told me what is right with me. Help me to gain a greater and greater revelation of who I am in Christ.*

## June 2

### DON'T FELLOWSHIP WITH MISERY

*Y*ou've heard it said, "Misery loves company." I say to you that this is true. Misery loves the company of self-pity, depression, frustration, anger, apathy, complacency, and other spirits that you have no business fellowshipping with. Misery loves company, but I will not fellowship with misery. Misery has no place in My presence. In My presence there is fullness of joy, fullness of peace, fullness of power, fullness of everything you need. Move away from misery and into My love, and you'll have a new outlook.

ROMANS 12:2; ROMANS 15:13; PROVERBS 17:22

### ✦ PRAYER ✦

*Misery is certainly miserable, and I've spent too much time in that place during my life. Help me to avoid this snare of the enemy. Help me avoid the trap of self-pity, apathy, complacency, and the other little foxes that spoil my vine. Help me shake off all of this and enter Your presence.*

## DISSECTING THE CULPRIT ATTACKING YOUR MIND

**O**UTSIDE FORCES WORK on your emotions more than you realize. Joy is not circumstantial for the child of God. Supernatural peace is not based on the situations you encounter as a child of God. Strength to rise up and battle against what's battling against you is always available for the child of God. Learn to pay close attention to the emotions you are feeling and realize they started with a thought. Trace your thoughts back to the culprit, and you will see what is robbing your joy, peace, and strength. Then cast it down and declare the opposite. Then teach others to do it so they too can be led by the Spirit and not by their souls.

PHILIPPIANS 4:6–7; ROMANS 12:2; ROMANS 8:5–6

### ⇥ PRAYER ⇤

*My thoughts shape my life. Therefore, help me guard my mind. Help me guard my heart, for out of it flow the issues of my life. Help me catch the enemy's subtle whispers before they take root in my heart. Help me reject the wicked notions the enemy suggests and hold on to Your Word.*

*June 4*

## Act Like Who Jesus Says You Are

$\mathcal{D}$o not allow yourself to be deceived into thinking, talking, and walking as someone you are not. You are the righteousness of God in Christ Jesus. Consider what that means. It means you are in right standing with Father. It means you can boldly approach the throne of grace to find grace and obtain mercy to help you in a time of need—any time and for any need. It means that you can petition Father for His will to come to pass in your life in faith and receive by faith His very best for you. Think, talk, and walk in the revelation and reality of who you are in Christ.

2 Corinthians 2:5–11; Hebrews 4:16;
Ephesians 2:10

### ✦ Prayer ✦

*I know who I am in Christ, but I need a deeper knowing. I need a knowing that guards me from even momentary feelings of condemnation. I need a knowing that helps me receive Your love, Your grace, Your mercy, and anything else I need in the moment. Please give me that knowing.*

## STOP LISTENING TO THE DEVIL'S PROPHECIES

SATAN IS THE father of all lies. He's been lying since the beginning. So why do you listen to his voice? Why do give thought to the worries he whispers to your soul? Why do you give ear to the fearful prophecies he declares over your life? You know My voice and you need not listen to any other. Read the Word. Confess the Word. Declare the Word. Proclaim the Word. Decree the Word. Prophesy the Word. Do not turn to the right or to the left. Stay on the narrow path of truth, and you will gain victory in the battle against your mind.

JOHN 8:44; 2 TIMOTHY 1:7; MATTHEW 7:13–14

### ❖ PRAYER ❖

*Your questions reveal my weaknesses. Thank You for confronting my heart with the truth and giving me instruction on how to walk in victory. Please remind me to decree, declare, and proclaim Your will over my life despite what I see, feel, and hear to the contrary.*

## June 6

## THE MISSING INGREDIENT IN YOUR REST

THERE'S A MISSING ingredient in your recipe for rest. You have neglected to cast all your cares on Christ, the one who cares for you. You have not leaned into Me and allowed Me to comfort you the way I long to. Take a step of faith now and begin to unload your burdens. Exchange them for My yoke, My love, and My anointing. Do you want what I am offering you? You first have to give up those things I never gave you or intended for you to carry. Then and only then can you pick up the things I have waiting for you.

EXODUS 33:14; MATTHEW 11:28–30; PSALM 127:2

### ✦ PRAYER ✦

*Thank You for revealing the missing ingredient in my rest. I will be careful to cast all my cares upon Jesus. I'd rather carry Your yoke, Your love, and Your anointing than my cares. Remind me to do this quickly. Remind me to do it fully— and help me not to take those cares back again.*

## Discerning the Difference Between Conviction and Condemnation

*L*ove is what separates religion from relationship. Love is the dividing line between conviction and condemnation. Knowing the love of God helps you know the difference between My conviction, which leads you to repentance and freedom, and the enemy's condemnation, which leads you into guilt and shame. I am for you. I love you. The wicked one is against you. He hates you. The enemy will work overtime to get you into works of the flesh and then condemn you when you fail. I will lead you to walk in the Spirit and prepare you for victory.

Romans 8:1; Romans 8:38–39; Galatians 5:16

### ☀ Prayer ☀

*It's all about love, isn't it? At the end of the day, it's all about love. Help me to receive Your love and Your conviction—and to reject the enemy's condemnation. I know Christ is not condemning me. I know I am forgiven when I run to Father.*

## June 8

## You Will Run With New Strength

*B*ECAUSE OF THE hunger of your heart, because of the desire of your soul, because you refuse to give up, I am sending winds of refreshing. I am pouring out a new anointing. I am igniting a fire in you that will act as a hedge of protection against the enemy's flaming missiles. You will hear the accusations, you will hear the imaginations, but the fire within you will be greater than the hell coming against you. You will run with new strength in this season.

PSALM 34:7; EPHESIANS 6:16; PSALM 23:3

### → PRAYER ←

*Thank You that You've made me hungry.
You've made me thirsty. You've stirred my
heart with Your great love. Help me to let my
light shine and my fire burn even in the dark
places. Help me to spread the fire of Your
love to everyone I come in contact with.*

# Nothing Frightens Me or Worries Me

*N*OTHING IS TOO hard for Me. Nothing frightens me or worries Me. Nothing puzzles me or stumps Me. Nothing is beyond My ability to restore, reconcile, or rescue. Believe Me and cast your cares on Me. I am waiting for you to roll your cares on Me so I can get to work on what's working against you. I am waiting for you to trust Me with the matters on your mind so I can bring you peace that passes your understanding.

JEREMIAH 32:17; JOEL 2:25–32; 1 PETER 5:7

### ✦ PRAYER ✦

*I love that nothing frightens or worries You. Nothing is impossible with You. Show me the way to finding faith in these truths. Show me how to lean all the way into Your heart. Show me how to root unbelief out of my soul so that I will not be concerned with anything but doing Your will.*

## June 10

### Wait With an Expectant Heart

*P*ATIENCE IS A virtue. Learning to wait is something of an art. Waiting with a heart expecting to see Me move in your life will breed peace in your soul. The enemy likes to attack in times of waiting. He wants to steal your peace that passes all understanding, steal your joy that gives you strength to fight the good fight, and steal your hope that undergirds your faith. He ultimately wants to replace the trust in your heart with doubt that makes My promises of no effect. How you wait is important. Be expectant. Remember to keep the eyes of your heart on the One who paid the price for every promise. Keep your eyes on Christ while Father handles your circumstances.

ROMANS 12:12; ROMANS 8:24; PSALM 27:13–14

#### ✦ PRAYER ✦

*I want to wait well. I want to wait with*
*expectancy and with hope, faith, joy, and*
*patience. Would You help me to keep my eyes*
*on Jesus? Would You draw me close so that*
*I can walk in peace while I wait? If You give*
*me the grace, I know I can run this race.*

## Don't Even Think About Lack

*L*ACK HAS NO place in your life. Lack should not be in your vocabulary. Father desires that you prosper and be in health, even as your soul prospers. So let your soul prosper. Meditate on the Word day and night—and be careful to do all it says—and then you will find good success. Speak the Word out of your mouth in agreement with the High Priest of your confession, and watch the Word do its work. Father's Word never fails. His Word does not return to Him void but accomplishes what it is sent to do. Send the Word into your circumstances. Then, only believe. You will see prosperity manifest in every area of your life.

3 JOHN 2; JOSHUA 1:8; HEBREWS 4:14

### ⤳ PRAYER ⤝

*Your Word is truth, and Your intentions toward
me are kind. Therefore, I reject any notion of
lack in any area of my life. You have called me
to have prosperity in my spirit, soul, and body.
Show me if I am doing anything that is hindering
Your good, perfect, and acceptable will in my life.*

## June 12

### MY PROMISES ARE YES AND AMEN

*I* ALWAYS KEEP My promises. I am not a man that I should lie, or a son of man that I should repent. When I speak to your heart, when I tell you I am going to do something, when I show you things to come, you can count on Me to do my part—and you can count on Me to prepare you to rise up and take hold of the promises. Consider the past promises I've made to you that have already come to pass, and let those victories and blessings encourage your heart. Remember when I've come through for you and showed Myself strong in your life. Let those memories make you brave. I'm with you—*still* with you.

NUMBERS 23:19; 1 SAMUEL 17:37;
2 CORINTHIANS 1:20

### → PRAYER ←

*You are a promise-keeper. All of Your promises are yes and amen. Help me to truly believe that. Give me the grace to meditate on Your Word until it renews my mind so that when I release my prayers, my faith will carry them to Father's ear. He will answer swiftly.*

## Remember This in the Silent Seasons

*J*ust because you don't hear My voice doesn't mean I am not with you. Just because you don't see Me moving doesn't mean I'm not working all things together according to the counsel of Father's will. Just because things look like they are growing worse instead of better doesn't mean that they won't get better. Remember, you are called to walk by faith and not by sight. You are called to trust a God you cannot see. You are called to stand and withstand. You are called to persevere through all adversity. And you are well able to do these things. Just because you don't hear My voice doesn't mean I'm not with you. Remember that in the silent seasons.

2 Corinthians 5:7; 1 Peter 5:10;
2 Corinthians 12:9

### ✦ Prayer ✦

*Teach me how to rely on Your Word even when I can't discern Your presence. Teach me to stand in the midst of the trial even when it feels like You are miles away. Teach me to understand Your ways and trust in You even when I can't see what You are doing.*

*June 14*

## I Direct Your Times and Seasons

WHAT DISAPPOINTS YOU doesn't disappoint Me. What surprises you doesn't surprise Me. What frustrates you doesn't frustrate Me. What discourages you doesn't discourage Me. Understand and know that I will direct your times and seasons. I direct your steps. I order your life. As long as you continue to lean and depend on Me and not on your own understanding, wisdom will be your guide. When you feel disappointed, shocked, frustrated, angry, upset, confused, discouraged, or ready to give up, lean on My strength, receive My comfort, and expect My help. I'm always ready with an answer. Calm your soul and listen for My next step.

PROVERBS 16:9; PSALM 37:23; PROVERBS 20:24

### ✦ PRAYER ✦

*I choose this day to lean on You. I choose this day to depend on You. I choose this day to walk in Your Word. Help me to stand fast on that commitment when my emotions are raging against the truth. Help me not to give into the feelings that would cause me to flee from Your heart.*

## LET ME HELP YOU IN YOUR WEAKNESS

*M*ANY PEOPLE HAVE knee-jerk reactions when people say or do things they don't like—or when bad things happen to them in life. Let your knee-jerk reaction be prayer. When prayer becomes your immediate response, it guards your heart from the anger, disappointment, and other emotions that are trying to lead you and guide you. Let Me lead you and guide you through your spirit. Let Me help you in your weakness when you pray. Turn immediately to Me, the Spirit of grace, to find the strength and wisdom you need to respond instead of react. You do that by prayer.

JAMES 1:19; PROVERBS 4:23; ROMANS 8:26

### ⬦ PRAYER ⬦

*Your wisdom never ceases to amaze me. Your wisdom is pure and perfect. I will apply it to my life in every season. Help me remember to ask You for the help I need. Remind me to turn to You right away before I react to people. Show me how to walk in love in my responses.*

## My Voice Should Be the Loudest

MY VOICE SHOULD be the loudest voice you hear. There are many voices in the spirit realm. Most of them are releasing fear, anxiety, depression, discouragement, and other ungodly thoughts that are not in My heart for you. Cast down those voices. Refuse to allow the lies into your heart. Listen for My voice. I am speaking to you more than You know, and I have the words of life. Keep your eyes and ears open. Look and listen for Me.

1 Corinthians 2:10; John 10:27;
2 Corinthians 10:5

### ✦ Prayer ✦

*I agree with You. Voices of doubt try to rob me of my faith. Voices of fear try to kill my faith. Help me tune in to Your voice so clearly that every other voice is just background noise.*

## Your Prayers Contain Tremendous Power

There's a good reason Jesus wants you to pray for those who hurt you, wound you, or viciously attack and malign you. Yes, there's a strategy behind this command that's intended to set you free from stress and emotional turmoil. There's a tactic within this directive to keep your heart clean of resentment, bitterness, and unforgiveness. Father's plans are perfect, and Christ died so that you not only could get free but also stay free. Praying for those who wrong you is a sure way to stay free, and it also helps the ones who wrong you find My will for their lives. Your prayers contain tremendous power.

Luke 6:28; Matthew 5:44; James 5:16

### ✦ Prayer ✦

*You always have my best interests at heart. I am so grateful for Your watchful eye. Please give me the grace to forgive those who hurt me, wound me, and attack and malign me—immediately. Help me not to harbor hard feelings in my heart. Help me pray for those who hurt me.*

## GET READY FOR YOUR KAIROS TIME

THERE IS A *kairos* time for you—more than one. There is a seasonable opportunity for everything in your life. My perfect timing is just that—perfect. Rather than trying to push your way into the new thing you sense that I want to do, prepare yourself and wait for My directive. I will make it very clear to you when your *kairos* is coming and lead you and guide you into the center of the right season. Your job is to pray, study your Bible to show yourself approved, and otherwise get yourself ready to walk in the fullness of what I have in store for you. There is a *kairos* time coming for you—more than one.

ECCLESIASTES 3:1–8; PSALM 31:14–15;
1 CHRONICLES 12:32

### ⟶ PRAYER ⟵

*I am ready for my kairos time—or at least I think I am. You know best. Show me how to prepare my heart and my mind for what You have planned for me. Stir my heart to study the Word and pray more and more. Get me ready to take the next step toward my destiny.*

## Forever Hope in God

WHEN THINGS DON'T turn out the way you expected, turn to Me. I'll be expecting you, and I'll be ready with the comfort and counsel you need in the moment. When life and people disappoint you, turn to Me. I will never disappoint you. As it is written in Romans 10:11, those who put their hope in God will never be put to shame. When you feel like everything that can go wrong has gone wrong, and you don't see an end in sight, turn to Me. I will show you the right way to go. I see the end from the beginning, and I will show you the way through and out. Always remember that I am right by your side at all times. You can turn to Me at any time with anything, and I will help you. That's a promise.

ROMANS 10:11; ISAIAH 46:10; ROMANS 15:13

### ✦ PRAYER ✦

*I will not just turn to You; I will run to You.
Make Your presence known to me. Illuminate
Your promises in my heart. Stir hope again
in my spirit. Cause me to release prayers
mixed with faith when everything looks like
it's about to blow up in my face. Help me.*

## June 20

### Your Life Is Marked by Glory

*A*RISE AND SHINE. My glory rests upon you. You may not see the glory when you look in the mirror every morning. You may not feel the glory as you walk through your day. You may even have a hard time believing it. But My glory is upon you. I am with you. My favor is upon you. My grace is upon you. My mercy is upon you. So rise up each morning and burn and shine for Me. Let the world know that Jesus is alive. Let your enemies see that nothing can stop you. Let your family witness that your life is marked by glory. Indeed, goodness and mercy shall follow you all the days of your life. Invite others into My glory.

ISAIAH 60:1; JOHN 17:22; 2 CORINTHIANS 3:18

### → PRAYER ←

*I believe Your words. I am ready to burn and shine for You. I am ready to glorify Christ with my life. I am willing to demonstrate that Jesus is alive and glorious. Teach me how to let His light and glory shine through me. Show me what to say and do everywhere I go.*

## TRUST IS THE PATHWAY TO PEACE

RUST IS THE pathway to peace, for there is no fear where trust exists. Love breeds trust, and perfect love casts out all fear. Trust in Me with all your heart, and lean not on your understanding. In all your ways acknowledge Me, and I will direct your steps. Trust Me to lead and guide you every step of the way into a broad place of blessing where you can come to know Me in a new way. I want to encounter you today and every day. Trust that I am with you always, and look for My blessings.

PROVERBS 3:5–6; PSALM 37:4–6; PSALM 31:8

### ⇒ PRAYER ⇐

*You are trustworthy. You are not a man that You should lie or a son of man that You should repent. All of Your promises are yes and amen. Help me shake off fearful thoughts that move me off Your promises.*

## June 22

### THE ENEMY IS UNDER YOUR FEET

*R*OCK BOTTOM IS where you feel like you've landed, but in reality you are seated in heavenly places with Christ Jesus even now. You are far above all principalities, powers, and problems. You are blessed. You are healed. You are victorious. You are prosperous. Look at what belongs to you in Christ and soar to new heights in Him. The enemy is under your feet. Remember these truths. Walk in hope, faith, and love.

EPHESIANS 2:6; EPHESIANS 1:3;
1 CORINTHIANS 13:13

### → PRAYER ←

*Thank You for reminding me that my feelings are not always the reality. Thank You for encouraging me when I feel down in the dumps. Please remind me to encourage myself in the Lord as David did. Teach me to offer the sacrifice of praise.*

## This Will Transform Your Relationships

A kind word of encouragement is more powerful than criticism. A loving tone will get you further than condemnation. Pray for a gentle spirit. Jesus said people would know His disciples by the love they have for one another. Check your heart. Are you walking in love with the people around you? Sometimes it takes a lot of grace to love people with unlovely behavior. But I assure you, God's grace is sufficient if you truly receive it. Receive His love and pour it out to others. Go on a criticism fast and compliment people instead of criticizing them. You'll be amazed at how this transforms your relationships.

Titus 3:2; 2 Timothy 2:24–26; Galatians 5:22–23

### ✦ Prayer ✦

*Help me remember to watch my tone and body language when I speak. Show me a way to communicate even difficult issues with love. Teach me how to season my speech with Your grace so people will truly hear my words.*

## June 24

### I'VE GIVEN YOU POWER
### AND A SOUND MIND

THE SPIRIT OF fear is rising. It's rising in this hour. The temptation to fear will rise along with it. But I have not given you a spirit of fear, as 2 Timothy 1:7 says. I've given you a spirit of love, and perfect love casts out all fear. I've not given you a spirit of fear; I've given you a spirit of power to overcome every spiritual enemy. I've not given you a spirit of fear; I've given you a sound mind that recognizes the subtle attacks against who you are in Christ. So meditate on My love. Receive My power. Know that you have the mind of Christ. And refuse to bow to the spirit of fear.

1 JOHN 4:18; PROVERBS 29:25; ROMANS 8:15

#### ⇢ PRAYER ⇠

*I will not fear. I refuse to fear. I stand against fear in every single one of its wicked manifestations. I will not bow to it or give its voice any room in my soul. Help me to stand strong against feelings of fear. Teach me how to discern its subtleties so I can rise above it.*

## Live by Faith in the Son of God

*J*ESUS IS ALIVE and has given you eternal life. In light of this, consider your ways. Are you living fully for Him? Are you enjoying all the benefits of a life devoted to His heart? Like Paul the apostle wrote in Galatians 2:20: "I have been crucified with Christ. It is no longer I who live, but Christ who lives in me. And the life I now live in the flesh, I live by faith in the Son of God, who loved me and gave Himself for me." Purpose in your heart to let Christ's life shine through yours. Draw on the Spirit of Christ within you to overcome every obstacle. Press into the work of the Cross. Know what belongs to you and fully surrender.

HAGGAI 1:5; MATTHEW 16:24; GALATIANS 2:20

### ❖ Prayer ❖

*I want to let my light shine. I want to burn and shine for You. Teach me how to draw upon Your Spirit for the light and life I need to keep the fire of Your love burning strong in my soul. Set me on fire and teach me how to spread that fire with wisdom.*

## I Am Working It All Out Right Now

*I* KNOW YOU'VE READ this many, many times before—you've even memorized Romans 8:28. But let me put you in remembrance of it anyway: *Father works all things together for good to those who love Him and are called according to His purpose.* That reality doesn't always make sense to your natural mind, but when you trust with your heart, you will begin to discern My hand working in even the most trying times of life. If you will be as diligent to seek Me as you are to talk about what the enemy is doing in your life, then you'll gain strength in the battle.

PROVERBS 3:5; PSALM 56:3–4; PSALM 13:5

### ⇥ PRAYER ⇤

*Kingdom realities are greater than natural realities. Help me understand kingdom principles and how they really work. Show me by Your Word and by Your Spirit how to move in the supernatural realm that defies reasoning. Give me a diligent heart that seeks You.*

## ALWAYS AGREE WITH ME

You don't have to agree with everybody about everything. But you need to agree with Me about everything, all the time. How can two walk together unless they agree? When you find yourself struggling to move along, wondering what to do and where to go, check to see if you are walking in full agreement with My heart. You may have slipped out of alignment in an area. The devil is roaming about like a roaring lion, seeking someone to devour. But he can't touch you when you are fully aligned with what I have told you to do. Be a doer of the Word.

Amos 3:3; 2 Corinthians 6:16; James 1:22

### → PRAYER ←

*I agree with You in my heart. It's my mind
that gives me trouble at times. Strengthen me in
my inner man so I can keep my soul and flesh
aligned with Your will. Help me to crucify my
flesh and keep it in submission to Your spirit,
even when it wants to war against Your goodness.*

*June 28*

## YOU CAN HAVE A NEW BEGINNING

*I*F YOU AREN'T getting off to the start you had hoped for earlier this year on New Year's Day, just start over again. Father is a God of second chances—and third, fourth, fifth, sixth, and seventh chances. You can have a new beginning—again. You can start over right this minute. You don't even have to wait until tomorrow. Don't let the devil complicate this. Let go of the past and move ahead. And if you fall down tomorrow, start over again the next day. Just keep asking Me for help along the way. You will overcome and fulfill your destiny. You *will* see victory!

ISAIAH 43:19; ROMANS 6:4; HEBREWS 12:1

### ✦ PRAYER ✦

*I'll take all the chances I can get! I need Your great grace. Show me the way of escape from my own failures. Help me overcome wrong tendencies, and when I do make mistakes, guard me from self-condemnation. Help me keep it simple.*

## Be Quick to Repent

You can't effectively pull down strongholds, cast down imaginations, and bring every thought into captivity without casting down in your mind every high thing that exalts itself against the knowledge of Me. In other words, when you are flowing in known sin, you are opening a door to the enemy that's hard to close. When I show you how you've missed the mark—when I convict you of wrong thoughts, words, or behavior—repent. Ask me for the grace of humility. Father resists the proud but gives grace to the humble. You need God's grace in the battle against your flesh.

2 Corinthians 10:5; Hebrews 12:1; John 16:8

### ❖ Prayer ❖

*I will pursue holiness—and I will run to Father as fast as I can when I miss the mark. I don't want to spend one moment apart from Your presence, so I will not let the enemy tempt me to run the other direction when I make a mistake. Give me the grace of humility.*

## June 30

### PRESS PAST THE RESISTANCE

THE RESISTANCE WILL only make you stronger. Press in. I am your strength and your shield. You will push back what is pushing against you if you don't let up. The kingdom of God suffers violence, and the violent take it by force. It takes energy to press past what is trying to hold you back, but the power that raised Christ from the dead dwells in you. I dwell in you. I abide in you. Abide in Me, and you will begin to notice the strength that's in your inner man. Abide in Me, and you will find that you are strong. You will find that you move in mighty power to break through what's trying to break you.

PSALM 28:7; EXODUS 15:2; NAHUM 1:7

### ⤞ PRAYER ⤝

*I am pressing in with everything in me—and I know I am growing stronger and stronger in Christ by the day. But some days the resistance is draining. Some days it's downright exhausting. Help me focus on the resurrection power that is within me and to appropriate Your sufficient grace to keep pressing past the resistance.*

# July

Now the Lord is the Spirit. And where the Spirit of the Lord is, there is liberty. But we all, seeing the glory of the Lord with unveiled faces, as in a mirror, are being transformed into the same image from glory to glory by the Spirit of the Lord.

—2 CORINTHIANS 3:17–18

## Choose Your Friends Wisely

Y ou never know someone until you watch how he behaves when he doesn't get what he wants from you. If someone has poor character, control issues, or other problems, saying no to him will cause him to manifest pride, rejection, or anger in a hurry. Saying no to someone with a controlling spirit will result in temper tantrums or accusations against you. Don't answer back. Bring it to Me, and ask Me what you need to do. I will show you a priceless lesson that will help you avoid close relationship with impatient people who see you as a tool to forward their goals.

Proverbs 13:20; 1 Corinthians 15:33;
Psalm 1:1

### → Prayer ←

*I wish all my friends were like You. You don't
try to manipulate me, and You never reject
me. Help me pick the right friends: friends with
proper motives, friends who have my best interest
at heart, friends who have Christlike character.
Help me avoid the ones who just want to use me.*

## July 2

### RESPONDING TO PRESSURE
### FROM ALL SIDES

WHEN PRESSURE MOUNTS on all sides, don't look to your right or your left. Father is trustworthy. He will deliver you. He may not show up immediately because He knows the pressure is useful for refining your character. But He will show up. He will send angels to fight for you if He has to. He will strengthen you to stand. When the enemy has convinced you that you are going to crack under the pressure, crack up laughing instead. Father laughs at His enemies—and you have this promise to stand on: when the enemy comes in like a flood, Father will raise up standard against him.

PSALM 34:17; HEBREWS 1:14; PSALM 2:4

### → PRAYER ←

*I want my character to be perfected. I know it's a process. Sometimes I don't know if the pressure is coming from the inside or the outside—and sometimes it feels overwhelming. But I know that You will guard and protect me. You won't allow more to come on me than I can stand.*

## Wait on Father to Vindicate You

*V*INDICATION IS SO sweet. The truth really does come out in the end. You don't need to defend yourself. God is your vindicator. He won't vindicate you as long as you are working overtime to vindicate yourself. Stop thinking about what people did to you. Stop reliving the past and think about the future and the hope Father has for you. While you're thinking about Him, He's working to set a table for you in the presence of your enemies. Be encouraged. Father sees what man has done to you, and He will repay you for your trouble.

ISAIAH 54:17; PSALM 135:14; ROMANS 12:19

### ✦ PRAYER ✦

*Oh, how I love Father's vindication. It is indeed sweeter than honey. Therefore, I resolve not to take matters into my own hands. Would You help me to wait for Father's perfect timing? Would You show me if I need to forgive? Would You prepare me for the blessings coming my way?*

## July 4

### DON'T TAKE IT PERSONALLY

WHEN SOMEONE LASHES out at you, don't let it hurt you. Don't take it personally. Don't think about what is right or fair or just. Don't even answer back. Stay silent in the face of your accusers. Leave the issue to Me. I will defend you. Take your focus off yourself. People who lash out at you are often hurting in some way. They are angry. They are afraid. Show compassion on those who lash out at you. Pity them because they are walking in misery and need the love of Father to invade their souls with peace and joy. Show them what love looks like. They need to see My love in action.

MARK 14:53–65; EPHESIANS 5:2; PSALM 18:1

### → PRAYER ←

*O Spirit of God, help me keep my big mouth shut when I am misunderstood. Help me to leave these matters where they belong—in Your capable hands. Teach me how to stand strong when I face the temptation to offer explanations or defenses, and give me a heart of compassion.*

## GUARD YOUR HEART FROM OFFENSE

*D*ON'T GET OFFENDED with Jesus when you are facing fiery trials. As Peter wrote, "Do not be surprised at the fiery ordeal that is taking place among you to test you, as though some strange thing happened to you" (1 Pet. 4:12). Trials are common to man, and you must trust your way through them. When John the Baptist was in prison facing death, Jesus sent him a message: "Blessed is he who is not offended because of Me" (Luke 7:23, NKJV). There is a blessing for the ones who don't get offended with Father in the face of tribulation. Don't fall for the devil's lies. Instead, rejoice in knowing Father is allowing the pressure to increase your anointing so you can help more people.

MATTHEW 11:6; 1 PETER 4:12;
2 CORINTHIANS 6:4–8

### → PRAYER ←

*I don't like going through trials. Teach me
how to trust my way through because it's
easier said than done when my feet are to the
fire. Teach me how to resist the spirit of offense
that tries to tell me You don't care. Help me
guard my heart from the enemy's wiles.*

*July 6*

## I Will Show You When to Transition

When it's time to move on, it's time to move on. But don't let the devil push you out of a position Father has ordained. Don't abort the mission. Don't let go of what Father has given you to steward no matter how hard holding on might be. There is a time to go and a time to stay; a time to give up and a time to press in harder; a time to rest and a time to run to the battle line. I will show you what to do, but you have to be willing to do My will. When you are willing to do My will, it will be easier for you to hear Me and move out—or stay on—in faith.

1 Peter 4:10; Colossians 3:23; Ecclesiastes 3:8

### ✦ Prayer ✦

*I tend to stay longer than I am supposed to, but You know that. I'm just trying to be careful because I don't want to hurt people or miss Your will. Help me to discern Your timing. Help me to recognize the winds of transition blowing in my life. I am willing.*

## Keep Talking to Me

When you hear Me speaking plainly, take that step of faith and keep your eyes on the prize. Keep looking ahead. Don't look back. Don't look to the right or to the left. That's where the distractions lie. Continue looking at Jesus, who gave you the faith you have to get where He wants you to go. Continue the conversation with Me. I will direct and redirect your steps if I have to. I won't let you stray from the narrow path that leads to the eternal rewards. I won't let go of your hand as you go on the journey that you call *life*. I won't slumber or sleep, even while you rest. I will guard you and keep you when you walk with Me.

Psalm 16:8; Proverbs 4:27; Isaiah 52:12

### ⤍ Prayer ⤎

*My mind wanders at times. Help me stay focused on what matters. Teach me how to incline my ear to Your voice in every situation. I am so grateful that You keep a watchful eye on me. Help me keep a watchful eye on You so I can follow You closely.*

## July 8

### RESPONDING RIGHTLY TO MISUNDERSTANDINGS

*T*HERE ARE TIMES in life when you will be misunderstood. There is no way to completely avoid misunderstandings, so you'll need to face that reality and prepare your heart to respond rightly in the face of misunderstanding. Decide now how you will respond when someone attacks you for something he thinks you did wrong, though your heart's motive was completely right. Yes, there are times when you should try to explain your side. But there are times when you need to just stay quiet and let Me work it out. I hold the hearts of men in my hands. Ask me for discernment when to speak and when to remain silent.

EPHESIANS 4:26; PROVERBS 21:1; MATTHEW 5:9

### ✦ PRAYER ✦

*Prepare my heart with a revelation of Your love, for it is Your unfailing love that will keep me through painful misunderstandings. Remind me to check my own heart motives and find even the smallest measure of truth in what people may say so I can grow in Christ.*

*Evenings With the Holy Spirit*

# HAVING ME WITHIN YOU GIVES YOU THE ADVANTAGE

*M*Y WILL IS stronger than your unsettled emotions. Choose to align your will with My will, and your unsettled emotions will have to bow to your spirit man. You know all too well that you are a spirit, you have a soul, and you live in a body. You are not meant to be ruled by your mind, will, imagination, emotions, or reasoning any more than you are meant to be ruled by your flesh. Build yourself up in your most holy faith, and let your spirit man lead the way. Having Me living in your spirit gives you an advantage over roller-coaster emotions and angry flesh that wants its way. Pray in the Spirit. Renew your mind. Crucify your flesh.

JUDE 20; 1 CORINTHIANS 14:15; ROMANS 12:2

### ⟶ PRAYER ⟵

*My will is strong, but it's not as strong as Yours.*
*You are immovable. Help me to see anything*
*in my heart that would choose not to fully*
*align with Yours. Help me rise up in my spirit*
*man and follow You with complete abandon.*
*Lead me, guide me, and prompt me to pray.*

*July 10*

## LEARN TO DISCERN MY
## SUPERNATURAL PEACE

*L*EARN TO SENSE the peace in your heart. You won't know it's missing if you don't know it's there. Peace belongs to you. Jesus left you His peace—not as the world gives it—but a supernatural peace that passes all understanding. That peace guards your heart and calms your mind. When you learn how to discern that peace, you won't want to do anything to jeopardize that peace. You'll guard it like a treasure. When that peace is missing, ask Me to show you what's wrong and how you can get it back again. You may need to repent, or you may be facing an enemy attack. Peace is a powerful weapon against the enemy!

2 THESSALONIANS 3:16; ISAIAH 26:3; 1 PETER 3:11

### ✦ PRAYER ✦

*I know You wouldn't tell me to learn something*
*You aren't willing to teach me. So I ask You*
*sincerely, would You teach me to let Your peace*
*be the umpire in every life situation I face?*
*Would You help me discern Your peace—not the*
*world's peace or soulish peace, but Your peace?*

*Evenings With the Holy Spirit*                    201

## MAGNIFY JESUS IN YOUR LIFE

When the Israelites focused on the giants in the Promised Land, they grew smaller in their own sight. They felt like tiny grasshoppers compared to the towering figures who possessed the land. They did not see how they could possibly defeat the opposing armies. Focusing on the giants made them fearful, and they were displeasing to Father, for without faith it's impossible to please Him. What you focus on affects your faith. If you keep your eyes on Jesus, your faith will grow. If you meditate on the Word, your faith will soar. Purposely choose to magnify the Lord, and you will overcome the giants that are standing guard over Father's promises for you.

NUMBERS 13:33; PSALM 34:3; ROMANS 10:17

### → PRAYER ←

*I don't want to believe an evil report. Help me see myself in Christ. Help me see myself as You see me. Help me overcome the fear that attacks my mind when I face new enemies—or old enemies that have come around in a more opportune season. I will magnify the Lord.*

## July 12

### Be Grateful for Your True Friends

**B**E THANKFUL FOR your trusted friends. Pray for them. Praise God for them. Open your heart to them. This is part of Jesus manifesting Himself in your life. You may have only a few genuine friends during your lifetime—friends who will walk with you through thick and thin, friends who will have your back no matter what, friends who will understand your heart and stand with you in the storms of life—but just a few is all you really need. And remember, Jesus is a friend who sticks closer than a brother. Seek to be a friend of God, and befriend those who need to know Jesus.

JOHN 15:15; JAMES 2:23; JOHN 15:13

### ✦ PRAYER ✦

*I am grateful—oh, so grateful—for the true friends You have brought into my life. Help me to steward these precious gifts well because it glorifies You when I cherish what You have given me. And thank You for being the ultimate friend who always understands my heart.*

## A Delay Is Not a Final Decision

*I*T'S JUST A delay; it's not the final decision. It's just a minor matter of waiting sometimes—and many times that minor matter can save you a lot of heartache in the end. Sometimes you think you are ready to do something, to have something, to go somewhere—but I know what is best for you. Don't be so quick to battle against an enemy every time you see a delay. Relax. Rest in Me. Ask Me for My perfect timing, and then let go and trust Me. That way, when your answer finally arrives, you'll be able to hold on to the victory and glorify your Father in heaven.

HEBREWS 4:10; 2 PETER 3:9; HABAKKUK 2:3

### ＋ PRAYER ＋

*Your timing is perfect. Help me to understand what You are saying so that I don't try to rush ahead of You or get frustrated when I don't see prayer answers as soon as I'd like. Give me the grace to wait for Your perfect timing in all things so that I can walk in Your perfect will.*

## Your Attitude Is Your Choice

Attitude is a decision of your will. You can choose to have a joyful demeanor. You can choose to walk in peace. You can choose to maintain a calm heart. You can choose to pursue a fiery love walk—even with your enemies. You have a free will. You can make the decision to walk in power, or you can walk in self-pity. No one can take control of your attitude, not even Me. So don't blame others for your outlook—but look up toward Me. When you feel your attitude deteriorating, start praising Jesus. Start worshipping Father. Start rejoicing in Me.

Philippians 2:14–15; Psalm 150;
1 Thessalonians 5:16

### ⊹ Prayer ⊹

*I agree with You. I am responsible for my own attitude. Please forgive me for choosing to grumble when I should be rejoicing. Help me to see things from Your perspective. Remind me to turn on the praise when the world seems to be turning on me.*

## JUDGE YOUR THOUGHTS

*Y*OU ARE FAR too tough-minded to give in to the imaginations the enemy is pushing on your soul. You have the mind of Christ! You are far too savvy to let the devil dump his garbage in your emotions. You have spiritual discernment and can judge all things. Start by judging your thoughts. If they don't line up with the Word, then don't give them a place in your soul. Don't let fearful imaginations—or imaginations of failure, rejection, or any other enemy ploy—stop you from moving ahead in Father's plan for you.

1 CORINTHIANS 2:15–16; 2 CORINTHIANS 10:5;
HEBREWS 4:12

### ☀ PRAYER ☀

*You are kind to me. I treasure Your encouragement. Give me greater revelation of the Word, which discerns between soul and spirit and judges the thoughts and attitudes of the heart. Help me judge my thoughts rightly according to Your words of life.*

## July 16

### RISE UP IN THE POWER OF HIS MIGHT

SOME DAYS YOU may feel down—and some days you may truly be downhearted. But you are never out. If you don't quit, you will win. If you don't give up, you'll get the victory. The truth is, you are not down at all but seated in heavenly places with Christ Jesus. That is your legal position in the kingdom. That means you are far above principalities, powers, and anything else that would try to drag you down. That means the devil is under your feet. So when you feel down, look up—don't give up. The devil is under your feet. Rise up in the power of His might and resume your position in Christ!

EPHESIANS 2:6; EPHESIANS 1:21; EPHESIANS 6:10

### → PRAYER ←

*I'm not a quitter, even though sometimes I do feel like throwing in the towel. Thank You for reminding me that I am victorious. Help me to see the big picture when the small details of life are trying to discourage me. Give me the grace to rise up and run!*

## You Will Witness Father's Delivering Power

ATHER HAS NOT forgotten about you. He already has your problems worked out. He had a solution for your problems before you ever ran into the challenge. He's ready and waiting for you to turn to Him and ask for help, in faith, believing that He will work all things together after the counsel of His will. He's waiting on you to petition heaven and seek justice and mercy. Sometimes you think you are waiting on Him when He's actually waiting on you. Lean on Him, not on your own understanding, and you will witness His delivering power in your life.

PSALM 107:6; 2 SAMUEL 22:2; PSALM 50:15

### ✦ PRAYER ✦

*Sometimes I'm stubborn. I try to do things in my own strength and wisdom. That doesn't usually work out very well. Help me remember to lean on Father instead of my own understanding. Prompt me to cry out for Your help when I need it.*

*July 18*

## REMIND YOUR ADVERSARY
## OF THESE TRUTHS

*W*HEN THE ENEMY comes knocking at your door with a package full of frustration and fear, don't accept the delivery. Remind your adversary that you have the peace of God, power, love, and a sound mind. Remind the wicked one that you are blessed with every spiritual blessing in heavenly places. Remind the devil that you are a partaker of Christ's divine nature and have everything pertaining to life and godliness. Remind your opponent you are more than a conqueror in Christ Jesus and that greater is He who is in you than he who is in the world. Your adversary will get so tired of hearing you confess the Word, he'll flee your doorway.

EPHESIANS 1:3; 2 PETER 1:4; ROMANS 8:31–39

### ⟶ PRAYER ⟵

*Thanks for reminding me! Yes, I will declare who I am in the face of the enemy's lies. I will proclaim that the Greater One lives in me. I will confess what Your Word says about me day and night. Please keep reminding me to do this when the adversary is attacking.*

## You Will Not Be Moved

THE RAINS WILL descend. The floods will come. The winds will blow. But when your life is founded on the Rock, you will not fall. It may feel as if your life is falling apart, but if you stand still, then you will see the salvation of your Father. So let the winds of adversity blow if they will. Let the rain of accusations fall upon you. Let the flood of fear take its best shot. You will not be moved because your faith is in Jesus. He is the author and finisher of your faith. He is able to make you stand amid the rainstorms, float on the floodwaters, and ride upon the wind.

MATTHEW 7:25–27; EXODUS 14:13;
HEBREWS 12:2

### ✦ PRAYER ✦

*I will not fear the rain, the floods, or the winds because You are with me. Help me to keep standing on the solid rock that is the revelation of Christ. Help me to rise up in faith when my circumstances look contrary. Help me use the opposition to my advantage.*

## July 20

### SWEET SLEEP BELONGS TO YOU

*T*OMORROW IS A new day. Let go of the pressure you carried this day and refuse to take on tomorrow's pressure before the sun rises. It won't do you any good at all to worry about tomorrow. Yes, tomorrow will have troubles of its own, but you can't tackle tomorrow's troubles today. And if you don't get some rest tonight, then you'll be ill-equipped to press through what tomorrow's circumstances throw your way. Father gives His beloved sweet sleep. So cast the worries on Him and rest well until morning. And when the sun does rise, have faith to believe that His grace is sufficient all day long.

MATTHEW 6:34; PSALM 127:2; PSALM 113:3

### ⇢ PRAYER ⇠

*I am grateful that Father's mercies are new every morning. I am grateful that I don't have to think about tomorrow's trouble today. Help me to toss it all aside and choose to rest in Your presence, confident in knowing that You will give me the grace I need to get through every tomorrow.*

## MEDITATE ON THE BEST

*Y*OU ARE MAKING everything worse by thinking the worst. Why not just believe Father for the best? Why plan and plot based on the bad news you expect to get? Instead, why not plan and plot based on the gospel? It is the *good news*. Meditating on negative things weakens the faith you need to carry your prayers to the throne of grace. Meditating on My truth will stir faith in your heart that will inspire you to go boldly before My throne and find the grace you need to deal with any situation—and you won't be tormented while you are waiting for Father to work it all out.

JOHN 8:32; EPHESIANS 6:14; 2 JOHN 2

### ✦ PRAYER ✦

*Love believes the best, and You love me—and You are love. So it's obvious that I should believe You. Help me think about who You are. Your character is flawless. You never back down from Your Word. You never break a promise. Your Word is truth, and it will set me free.*

*July 22*

## FOCUS YOUR STRENGTH
## ON PLEASING FATHER

*N*O MATTER HOW hard you try, you can't live up to everyone's expectations all the time. And if you did, they would just raise the expectation bar higher. Instead of working so hard to please man, focus your strength on pleasing Father. You will never do everything right as long as you are in that fleshly body, but you don't have to be perfect to please Father. You just have to set your heart to please Him and be quick to repent when you miss the mark. Pleasing God is actually a lot easier than pleasing many people. Indeed, Father will give you grace to press on—and He's much more forgiving than man.

1 JOHN 3:22; HEBREWS 13:16; HEBREWS 11:6

### ⤞ PRAYER ⤝

*I'm so glad I don't have to be perfect to please You, because I'm sure not perfect. You are so much more gracious than anyone I know. Teach me what pleases Your heart. Show me Your ways. Teach me Your paths. Tell me what delights You. That's all that ultimately matters to me.*

## PERSEVERE IN MY GRACE

**P**ERSEVERANCE CAN HELP you reach Father's will for your life faster—and this admirable quality will safeguard you from throwing in the towel when things become more difficult than you expected. Perseverance is not about works of the flesh. It's about following Me and doing what I tell you to do, when I tell you to do it, and how I tell you to do it. Your hard work alone is not enough. You must persevere in the grace of obedience to follow My instructions. Apart from Jesus you can do nothing. You can't make it without My grace. So persevere in your diligence and stay sensitive to My leading, and you will get there in My timing.

2 TIMOTHY 2:12; 2 THESSALONIANS 3:13;
HEBREWS 10:36

### ⟶ PRAYER ⟵

*I know I can't make it without Your grace. I need
Your grace to press through to the end. I need
Your anointing to break through the opposition.
Please fill me with Your Spirit anew. Help me
to follow Your instructions line by line and
precept by precept. Reveal Your perfect timing.*

## July 24

## DON'T BOW TO THE FALSE GOD OF FEAR

*I* KNOW THE SITUATION staring in your face is screaming for you to take action. I understand the voice of fear and its agenda. I know what it sounds like and how tempting it is to bow to that false god. But slow down and wait for your heavenly Father. He already knows how to work this out for good. Don't rush ahead of Him and make a bigger mess. He really will show you what to do if you just wait on Him. There's a difference between letting the voice of fear paralyze you into inaction and waiting on Father for a word of wisdom that will carry you through to a good outcome.

ISAIAH 41:10; PSALM 56:3–4; DEUTERONOMY 7:21

### ⇥ PRAYER ⇤

*Help me to stand strong against the voices of fear that tempt me to take matters into my own hands instead of waiting upon You to show me the way through. Help me to hear Your voice more loudly than any other voice competing for my mind's attention. I choose to follow Your voice.*

## Don't Be Afraid to Speak Up

If you tolerate sin against you because you don't want to offend anyone, then you are teaching people to mistreat you. You are telling them it's OK to abuse you. Don't be afraid to speak up when the sins against you are damaging or dangerous. Speak the truth in love and be willing to cut ties with those who are intent on bringing trouble, drama, and chaos into your life. I have healthy relationships for you, but sometimes you have to let go of the toxic ones to see them.

Matthew 18:15; Ephesians 4:15;
1 Corinthians 14:33

### → Prayer ←

*Give me the boldness mixed with grace to confront people in love who aren't acting loving toward me. Help me resist the pressure to allow people to consistently mistreat me. Give me discernment to find right relationships and draw back from toxic ones.*

## July 26

### CHOOSE TO GLORIFY JESUS

STOP DREADING THE rat race and make a
solid decision to glorify Jesus this week
in your home, your work, your school, and your
church. Wherever Father has placed you, remember
that you are serving Him, and He will reward you
for your diligence and faithfulness. Do everything
as you would do it for your heavenly Father, and
you will find joy even in the most mundane tasks.
Decide by your will to rejoice, to walk in peace,
and to demonstrate love. You are salt and light! I
am with you to empower you to walk in a manner
worthy of your calling.

COLOSSIANS 3:23; EPHESIANS 6:7;
PROVERBS 22:29

### ⋆ PRAYER ⋆

*I want my life to glorify Jesus—every aspect of
my life. Help me to adopt the mind-set that I
am serving Father as I serve others. Help me to
serve with excellence and to minister to others
the way You have ministered to me. Teach
me how to be a true ambassador for Christ.*

## Stand and Withstand

WHEN YOU FEEL like drawing back or giving up, recognize that the enemy is at work. Part of the enemy's strategy is to bring circumstances against your life and imaginations against your mind that cause you to get away from your post. You just want to quit. That's when you need to stand and withstand. Father is able to make you stand! Don't give the enemy the satisfaction of even slowing down—even if he knocks you down. Get right back up and run hard after Father's will for your life. I am with you. You can do this!

Matthew 11:12; 2 Corinthians 2:11; Philippians 1:28

### → PRAYER ←

*I will not be ignorant of the devil's devices, and I refuse to give him more power over my life than he really has. Thank You for exposing the wicked one's schemes against my life. Please help me to push back the darkness that tries to cloud my mind, will, and emotions. Help me stand.*

## July 28

### REMEMBER WHO YOU ARE IN CHRIST

*Y*OU ARE STRONG. You are bold. You are righteous. You are holy. You are wise. You are fearless. You are fierce. You are victorious. You are prosperous. You are healed. You are whole. You are favored. You are loved. You are all of these things and more in Christ. Put on Christ. Walk in Christ. Remember Christ when you rise up and when you lie down. As you think about who you are in Him, the reality of who He is in you will manifest more and more in your life.

PROVERBS 28:1; 1 PETER 1:16; ROMANS 13:14

### ✦ PRAYER ✦

*Thank You for reminding me who I am—who I really am in the eyes of Father through the blood of Jesus, through being in Christ. Help me keep my mind stayed on Him and what that means in every area of my life. Give me dove's eyes of devotion for my Beloved One.*

## SHAKE YOURSELF LOOSE

*D*ON'T ALLOW THE enemy to frame your tomorrow with your today—or the days before. Shake off the dust of today. Shake loose from the memories of yesterday and move into your tomorrows confident in who you are in Christ. Whether it was stress, sin, or sadness, shake it off and come up higher in Him. Repent, and change your thinking. If God is for you, who can be against you? Think about that for a minute. The world may hate you because it hates Christ, but if I am standing with you, what does it matter who hates you? No weapon formed against you can prosper— no matter who launches it.

MATTHEW 6:34; ROMANS 8:31; ISAIAH 54:17

### ⇢ PRAYER ⇠

*Help me shake myself loose from any ties that try to bind me. Show me how to shake loose of the worries and cares that try to choke the Word out of my heart. Teach me how to let go of the emotions that hold me back from the peace and joy You have ordained for me.*

## July 30

### KEEP YOUR SPIRIT SHARP

Sometimes the enemy blindsides you. It happens to everybody. Don't beat yourself up. Instead, learn to stay vigilant, remember to stay watchful, and always stay prayerful. When you take My advice in these matters, you will be able to see the enemy coming from a distance. Your enemy is always roaming around seeking for someone to devour. But when you gird up the loins of your mind, keep your spirit sharp, and remain in fellowship with the Me, you're less likely to be blindsided.

1 Peter 5:8; 1 Peter 1:13; 1 Thessalonians 5:17

### ✦ PRAYER ✦

*Help me not to put my spiritual guard down but to remain watchful and alert at all times. If I am doing anything that dulls my spiritual senses, please show me so I can direct my attention back to where it belongs. Help me stick close enough to You to hear Your slightest whispers.*

## WHAT DEVASTATES YOU DOES
## NOT DEVASTATE ME

*W*HAT DEVASTATES YOU does not devastate Me. Don't give in to the feelings of devastation that flood your soul when unexpected events in your life seem tragic. Father's Word is good, and His Word says He will work all things together for good for you because you love Him and are called according to His purposes. What looks to you like the end can be a new beginning. I will comfort your heart when you look to Me and trust in Me.

PSALM 39:7; ROMANS 8:24; PROVERBS 23:18

### → PRAYER ←

*I know the Word is true—and that nothing surprises You. Would You help me to respond to disappointment and devastation with an attitude of hope? Would You help me focus on what's good even in the midst of a storm? Let Your hope anchor my soul.*

# August

You must fear the LORD your God. You must
serve Him and cling to Him, and swear by
His name. He is your praise, and He is your
God, who has done for you these great and fear-
some things which your eyes have seen.

—DEUTERONOMY 10:20–21

## Expect Him to Move Mountains

*J*esus, the Son of the living God, is your deliverer. So despite whatever is holding you back, pressing you down, or shaking you up, cry out to your deliverer today and expect Him to set you free, send you forth, settle your heart, and answer your prayers. Expect Him to defend you, protect you, move your mountains, and work miracles in your life. Look for Him to make the wrong things right and even to work all those out for your good. Wait for it. You may wait longer than you want to, but the end is worth the wait.

2 Samuel 22:2; Psalm 50:15; 2 Peter 2:9

### ⸬ Prayer ⸬

*Jesus is my rock, my fortress, and my deliverer.*
*He is my strong tower. I will run into Him*
*and find protection and freedom. Help me to*
*expect Father's defense on my behalf. Help*
*me to wait on His delivering power. Help*
*me to build faith to move mountains.*

## Continue Walking
## Toward Your Future

*B*EWARE OF ASSOCIATIONS from the past who have come to spy out your liberty. Don't be ensnared again. Don't accept the yoke of bondage they want to lay around your neck to slow you down. Don't let smooth talkers bewitch you with flattery. Some will come throwing fiery darts from your past. Some will come telling you why you can't do what I've told you to do. Some will come with jealous intentions now that you are standing in My will. Continue walking toward your future, and stay free in Me!

GALATIANS 2:4; GALATIANS 5:1; PSALM 12:3

### → PRAYER ←

*Human nature is sad sometimes, but I am a partaker of Christ's divine nature. Help me to walk confidently knowing who I am. Teach me to discern the ones who are trying to bring me into legalism, hold me to my past, or flatter me with smooth sayings. Protect me from the jealous ones.*

## YOU DON'T NEED TO HAVE
## ALL THE ANSWERS

*W*HEN YOU KNOW something is wrong and you don't know what it is, pray in your heavenly language. Pray with Me. I know what is opposing you. It's no secret to Me. Nothing is hidden from My sight. I may choose to reveal to you what is operating so you can take authority over the opposition, or I may choose to send an angel to war on your behalf. It's not always necessary for you to know what is going on or why it is happening. It is important for you to trust Me and know that I have your back. Always.

ROMANS 8:26; EPHESIANS 6:18;
1 CORINTHIANS 14:15

### → PRAYER ←

*Even if I did know what was opposing me, I don't always know how to pray. I need Your strategies for victory. Teach my hands to battle and my fingers to war. Help me to trust You for the victory even when I cannot see what is going on in the spirit realm.*

## WHAT SEASON ARE YOU IN?

*D*o you know what spiritual season you are in right now? Do you know where you are headed? I do, and I want to prepare you to move in My perfect timing. Remember, Solomon wrote about times and seasons. There is indeed a time for every purpose under heaven. To everything there really is a season. Take some time to quiet your heart and ask Me what season you are in so you can respond accordingly. I will show you how to get ready for the new thing. I will ready you to let go of the old thing so you can stand in My perfect will.

ECCLESIASTES 3; DANIEL 2:21; PSALM 1:3

### ⁑ PRAYER ⁑

*What season am I in? Sometimes I think I know, but I will continue to ask You because seasons can shift suddenly and subtly. Would You help me prepare my heart for each shifting season? Would You help me stay ahead of the shift so I land in my next season ready to run?*

## My Way Is the Easiest Way

When something seems harder than it should be, or when you are frustrated with the same old issue that repeats itself over and over again, stop and think. Ask yourself this hard question and be honest with yourself: are you doing this Christ's way? Sometimes you don't know what Christ's way is. Sometimes you know, but you take a different route because you don't fully trust in your heavenly Father to stand by His Word. My way is the easiest way. It may not seem that way from where you sit, but I assure you that it is from where I stand.

Psalm 27:11; Psalm 86:11; Psalm 25:9

### ⊹ Prayer ⊹

*Your ways are higher than my ways. Would you teach me Your ways? Would you show me how You see, think, and feel about situations? Would You show me the easy way? I don't want to walk around the same mountain over and over on my way to the promised land.*

## August 6

### Trials Can Leave You With Wisdom

No one likes to go through the fire. No one likes to walk through the trials. I don't blame you. Jesus didn't like the shame of the cross and the pain He endured hanging on that tree. But know this: if you stay close to Me and keep an open line of communication with Me, the trial will leave you with wisdom that you couldn't have gotten any other way. You won't want to go through it again, but you will be glad you walked through that fire.

James 5:10–11; 1 Corinthians 10:13;
James 1:13–15

### → Prayer ←

*I need all the wisdom I can get, so I will embrace the journey, including the fiery trials, and seek to learn valuable lessons along the way. Please speak to my heart when I am in the fire. Please whisper Your truths in my ear when I am in the valley. Give me an enduring heart.*

## Your Prayer Answers Will Come in Like a Flood

*Y*ou've been waiting for many years to see some of your prayer answers. You have even forgotten about many of the fervent and passionate prayers you prayed long, long ago. Don't give up now. Hold on. I'm telling you, when you least expect it, those prayer answers will start coming in like a flood. First a trickle, and then a flood. When they do, be sure to thank Father before and after. He is working on your behalf.

Mark 11:24; John 15:7; 1 John 5:15

### ✦ Prayer ✦

*I've been contending and confessing, believing and asking, seeking and knocking. Thank You for reassuring me that the answers are on the way. Help me to keep an attitude of praise and thanksgiving while I wait for the deluge of prayer answers coming my way.*

## Remember, You Are Royalty

𝒴ou are a child of the Most High God, the Creator of heaven and Earth. You are a child of the One who heals, delivers, restores, prospers, and loves. You are a child of the everlasting God who was and is and is to come. You are a child of the King of kings and Lord of lords. That means you are royalty. See yourself through His eyes, and don't allow others to tear down what Jesus is building in you. Respect yourself. Love yourself.

1 Peter 2:9; Revelation 1:6; John 1:12

### ✦ Prayer ✦

*I am royalty. I am a child of a good, good Father. I am a king and priest in Christ. I have gifts, authority, and favor in heaven. Help me renew my mind to this way of thinking. Show me areas of my life where I am living below my identity in Christ. Help me see myself rightly.*

## Decide to Act Like Jesus

You can choose to act like Jesus did in the face of unfair treatment. It's not always an easy choice, but if you make a decision to be Christlike when you are mistreated, you will discover it is liberating. You will have peace in your spirit and soul when you walk in His way. Don't let evildoers from your past hold you in bondage. Don't let the accusers from your present hold you down. Forgive, and be free. Then go a step further: bless them, pray for them, and show them kindness.

Ephesians 5:1; 1 Corinthians 11:1;
Philippians 2:5

### → Prayer ←

*The Word says I live and move and have
my being in Christ, so I should be able to
demonstrate His character. Help me to cultivate
and manifest the fruit of Your Spirit in my life.
Help me to show the love of Christ to all people,
whether they are showing me love or hate.*

## August 10

### IT'S TIME TO PRESS!

*T*HIS IS A time to *press*. I know it seems too hard, you are too tired, and there is too much opposition—too much at stake. But Father is a God of more than enough—nothing is too much for Him. *Press!* It's up to you to resist the demonic pressure that's resisting your progress. *Press!* It's not always comfortable to plow ahead, but you can do it by God's grace! *Press!* If you choose not to press, then you will look back with regret. If you choose to press, then you will look back on victory. *Press!*

PHILIPPIANS 4:13; JOHN 16:33; JAMES 4:7

### ✦ PRAYER ✦

*I am determined to press past the resistance
and press on toward the prize of my high calling
in Christ. Please give me the strength to press
and keep on pressing. Help me press past my
own flesh when it rises up against Your Spirit,
and help me press pass demonic resistance.*

## What You Can Do in Christ

*I*N Christ you can put to death the deeds of the body before the deeds of the body put you to death. In Christ you can triumph over every single enemy. In Christ you can walk in love and supernatural peace. In Christ you can be truly free forever. In Christ you can be healed. In Christ you can do all things. Keep your mind on spiritual things and you'll overcome fleshly appetites as I empower you with My grace.

Romans 8:2; 1 John 5:18; Colossians 3:9–10

### ✦ Prayer ✦

*I am committed to the process of crucifying my flesh. I am committed to die daily. I am committed to picking up my cross and following Jesus. Help me back up that verbal commitment with determined action. Give me the grace to follow Christ all the days of my life.*

*August 12*

## You Can Send Confusion Into the Enemy's Camp

$\mathcal{U}$NDERSTANDING THIS TRUTH will help you in the midst of the battle. The devil is not really after your money, your job, or your family. He just goes after those things as a way to steal your joy. The joy of the Lord is your strength. Your joy is a weapon of warfare. Joy is a choice of your will, just like forgiveness. Choose today to rejoice despite what you see with your eyes and feel in your soul, and you will send confusion into the enemy's camp.

Nehemiah 8:10; Psalm 28:7; 2 Chronicles 20:22

### ✦ Prayer ✦

*Fill me with Your joy. Pour out Your joy over me. Let it wash over me like a river. Help me to choose joy in the face of discouraging life events. Help me walk in joy amid my trials. Help me make a joyful noise when I feel like complaining. Teach me to war with joy.*

## I Am Standing With You

*I* know sometimes it feels like you can't stand it anymore, but Father has not called you to live by your feelings. You are called to walk in Me. You are called to walk in the Word. The Word says when you've done all you can do, then stand. I know the battle is real. I know the fight is fierce. I'm in it with you. Father is able to make you stand. Don't give up. Don't let your emotions dominate your life. I am standing with you.

Galatians 5:16; Ephesians 6:13; Romans 14:4

### ✦ Prayer ✦

*I refuse to let my emotions dominate my will, my mind, or my spirit. Alert me quickly when I begin to slip over into the soulish realm. Show me right away when I am slipping into the flesh. Take hold of my hand, and lead me and guide me into the truth about the victory that belongs to me.*

## August 14

### WAIT FOR MY GREEN LIGHT

**D**on't engage in serious conversations until I give you a green light. Some will try to push the issue and insist that you talk, but if you wait on Me, I will give you the words to say in the right time. Practically speaking, sometimes you just need a time-out. If your efforts to smooth things over make the situation uglier, back off and pray. Let things settle before you engage in communication again. Pray for those who fired the darts, get godly counsel, and keep your shield of faith up. I will work it out. And if the relationship is truly ordained, then the test will make it stronger in the end.

LUKE 12:12; EPHESIANS 4:29; PROVERBS 11:14

### ✦ PRAYER ✦

*Set a guard over my mouth so that I will not speak out of turn. Show me Your perfect timing for critical conversations, and help me not to carry a defensive or accusatory demeanor. Help me to remember when I do speak that a soft answer turns away wrath.*

## DON'T ALLOW URGENCY TO LEAD YOU

*Y*OU OFTEN FEEL an urgency to respond to situations that arise, to put out the raging fire right now—immediately. But understand and know this: if you will slow down and wait on My leading, then many times you won't even have to address the situation. Try praying before taking action, and if you need to take action, I will lead you to make the right moves in My timing. I will give you wisdom on how to respond. Don't rush ahead of Me.

JAMES 1:5; JAMES 3:17; PROVERBS 3:13–18

### → PRAYER ←

*I know I run too fast sometimes. I don't like issues to linger. But help me to slow my step. Teach me how to bite my tongue, put my hands in my pockets, and wait until You say go. Let my first response to the fire be prayer. Give me a sense of Your timing and reveal Your strategy.*

## You Were Born Again for Breakthrough

You were born again for breakthrough. You were born again for victory. You were born again for triumph. Nothing can defeat you when you walk with Me. Nothing can hold you back from Father's perfect will when you follow My lead. No devil in hell can stop your destiny. You were born again for such a time as this!

Jeremiah 51:20; Mark 11:23; Esther 4:14

### ✦ Prayer ✦

*You are my breakthrough! Give me a breaker anointing so I can press past the things that stand in between me and my Father's will. Help me determine in my heart even now that I will not let man, devil, or beast stop me from doing what He has called me to do. Thank You for strengthening me.*

## I Am for You, Not Against You

*I* AM ABLE TO make you stand. When people are judging your heart, remember that I see who you really are. When people are lying about you, remember that I know the truth. When people are talking behind your back, remember that my thoughts toward you are good—and they are countless. When people hurt you, remember that I am your comforter and healer. When people don't understand you, remember that I created you, I know everything about you, and I love you. When you feel like there's nowhere to turn, turn to Me. I'm here. I always will be.

ROMANS 8:31; PSALM 118:6; PSALM 108:13

### ✢ PRAYER ✢

*Thank You for standing with Me and for Me. You are loyal and true. Help me to stand with You and for You. Help me to be faithful, true, and loyal to You all the days of my life. Help me not to compromise the Word of God or take Your Spirit for granted.*

# August 18

## Just Slow Down

Slow down. Take it easy. You are running so fast and so hard some days that you miss the finer points to life. You can't run faster than I do and expect Me to lead you. You can't get ahead of Me and still be following Me. You can't expect to hear My voice if you are not listening. You can't expect to see Me in your circumstances if you don't look. You can't expect to understand My ways when you are doing things your way. So take My advice. Slow down. Take a deep breath. Follow Me, listen for My voice, and watch for My blessings. Slow down.

Romans 12:2; Mark 6:31; Luke 10:38–42

### ✦ Prayer ✦

*I hear You loud and clear. Life is so busy, but I don't want to miss You. Please help me to move in Your grace and not beyond Your grace. Please help me to see You, hear You, and follow You all day, every day. I want to practice Your presence and discern Your heart.*

## Do Everything Unto the Lord

*Y*OU HAVE A generous spirit. I love that about you. Your generosity blesses many—but it blesses Me the most. Every time you give your time, share your counsel, spend your money, or just offer a smile and a kind word to someone who is having a bad day, it blesses Me. You are displaying My fruit when you show kindness. You are displaying My love when you sacrifice what you need or what you want in order to give someone else what he needs and what he wants. Remember this, when you do these things unto the Lord, there will be a great reward. Even if you share a cold cup of water with someone in Christ's name, rewards await.

COLOSSIANS 3:23; EPHESIANS 6:7;
GALATIANS 5:22–23

### → PRAYER ←

*It blesses me that You notice even the little things. I'm not doing it for the rewards, but I appreciate the principles of Your kingdom. Help me to notice the people around me who need help. Help me identify the needs—and help me to have and keep right motives.*

## NEVER SAY NEVER

NEVER SAY NEVER. You don't know the full counsel of My will. You don't know how things may pan out in the end. You don't know what things will look like in the middle— or how many new beginnings you'll enjoy in your life. You can think, pray, and plan, but remember that I am ordering your steps. I am working all things together after the counsel of My will. I am orchestrating your life. Stay sensitive to Me. Remain flexible on your journey. I will not only show you things to come, but I will also take you to them.

JAMES 4:15; PROVERBS 19:21; EPHESIANS 1:11

### → PRAYER ←

*I know I sometimes speak as if I know it all, but I submit my life to You. I submit my plans to You. I submit my steps to You. I submit everything that I have and everything that I am to You. Do with me what You will, and I will rejoice in Your leading all the days of my life.*

## Dwell On the Resurrected Christ

*I* know your past, and I know your future. But I am not looking at your past, and neither should you. Don't dwell on the trials, the pain, and the losses of days gone by. Dwell instead on the future and the hope Father has in His heart for you. Dwell instead on the resurrected Christ who lives inside of you. Dwell instead on My presence. Dwell on your eternity with us in the kingdom that never ends.

Isaiah 43:18; Philippians 3:12–14;
2 Timothy 2:8

### → Prayer ←

*Dwell is such a strong word. I am seeing that what I dwell on has power in my life. Therefore, help me dwell on Your love. Help me dwell on Father's Word. Help me dwell on the resurrected Christ. Teach me how to think about things with eternal value instead of the distant past.*

## STAY ON POINT

STAY ON POINT. Stay in your lane. Don't try to be something you are not. Don't compare yourself to others. Learn from them. Glean from them. But remember that I am your ultimate teacher, and I am forming you into the image of Christ. I am changing you from glory to glory. I have put a word in your mouth. Be faithful to share what I give you. Stay on point.

2 CORINTHIANS 3:18; ROMANS 8:29;
2 CORINTHIANS 10:12

### → PRAYER ←

*The world is full of pushes and pulls. Everybody wants something all the time and right now. People expect me to be something I am not. Help me to stay focused on the high call on my life in Christ Jesus. Give me wisdom in using the gifts Jesus has given me to glorify Him.*

## Take On an Abundance Mind-Set

Abundance. Father's kingdom is one of abundance. There is always more than enough. Don't allow scarcity to enter your mind. Don't allow fear of lack to enter your soul. Stop thinking about what you might not have and focus on what you do have. You have promises in the Word about provision and prosperity. You have Me dwelling inside you. You have eternal life awaiting you. You don't have to worry about tomorrow. You don't have to wonder where your provision is coming from. We have more than enough.

Deuteronomy 28:1–14; Ephesians 3:20;
John 10:10

### ⤖ Prayer ⤚

*You are a God of more than enough—and Father
is faithful to share His wealth with me. I have
all things pertaining to life and godliness. Help
me see what truly belongs to me. Show me the
riches of the glory that is in Christ Jesus. Teach
me to receive the good gifts available to me.*

## DON'T GO INTO TIME-DEBTS THAT STRESS YOUR LIFE

*Y*OU DON'T NEED to feel as if you owe everyone everything you have. People will take whatever you will give them. Take caution that you don't go into a time-debt that strains your life. Take caution that you don't give beyond what you have to give. You don't owe them your time. You don't owe them your friendship. You don't owe them your energy. Owe no one anything except to love them. You don't owe people anything beyond honor, respect, and love. You don't have to feel guilty when you say no.

ROMANS 13:7–8; EPHESIANS 5:2; JOHN 15:17

### ⤳ PRAYER ⤶

*That is truth that sets me free. You have given me a servant's heart. I want to honor others in all that I do, but I hear You saying I also need to honor my own needs. Thank You for helping me to see the other side. Give me guidance about when, how, and whom I serve.*

## I Have Given You Influence

*I*NFLUENCE. I HAVE given you a measure of influence, and I expect you to exercise that gift to bring people to a greater knowledge of Me. I have given you influence with your friends, with your family, and in your community. In fact, your influence extends beyond the borders you can see. Every person you influence ultimately influences someone else. So take care. Be mindful of your words and actions and how they impact the people around you. The ripple effect of your life will amaze you in eternity.

MATTHEW 5:13–16; PROVERBS 9:9;
1 THESSALONIANS 1:7

### ✦ PRAYER ✦

*Thank You for the trust You have shown
me. I know I represent Jesus in the earth and
that I have a responsibility to show forth His
love and make Him known. Help me use the
talents Father gave me to increase His kingdom.
Teach me to be a wise steward of my gifts.*

## I HAVE SO MUCH MORE FOR YOU

*Y*OU CAN NEVER get enough of Me. You can never get too much of Me. I will never hold Myself back from you when you seek Me with your whole heart. When you hunger and thirst after righteousness, you will be filled. When you determine in your heart to go after Me with everything in you, you will not only find Me, but you will also find My gifts, and My fruit will become more mature in your life. In My presence there is fullness of joy and everything else that you need.

DEUTERONOMY 4:29; PROVERBS 8:17;
JEREMIAH 29:12–14

### → PRAYER ←

*I would sit in Your presence all day if I could,*
*rejoicing in You. But the responsibilities of*
*life are demanding. Teach me how to practice*
*Your presence in the mundane activities of life*
*and with the important deadlines I face. Show*
*me how to walk in You all day, every day.*

## REPETITION IS YOUR FRIEND

**R**EPETITION IS YOUR friend. Repeat the Word over and over. Read it again and again. Talk about what you have learned. Share it with whomever will listen. Read books packed with the Word. Listen to messages that share the lessons. Get kingdom principles into your spirit when you wake up in the morning and as you go to sleep at night. Find creative ways to keep the Word in front of you. Meditate on the Word day and night, and then be careful to do all it says. Then you will discover your ways are successful.

2 TIMOTHY 3:16; JOSHUA 1:8; PSALM 119:97

### ✦ PRAYER ✦

*I'm inspired! I want to eat the scroll. I want to meditate on the Word day and night. I want it to become part of me. I want it to renew my mind completely. Let this inspiration motivate my heart to make the necessary changes in my life to keep the Word at the forefront of my life.*

## August 28

## The Key to Lasting Transformation

Tips and tricks will take you only so far. Kingdom principles will carry you where I want you to go. Exercise My kingdom principles and you will see kingdom fruit. Put in place kingdom principles and you will step into a new dimension of truth that makes you more and more free. Decide to abide by kingdom principles and you will see the change you want in any area of life in which you choose to follow Me. Tips and tricks are a quick fix. Kingdom principles and lessons are the key to lasting transformation.

Romans 14:17; Galatians 2:19–21;
Matthew 6:33

### ❖ Prayer ❖

*I agree with You. Kingdom principles—not self-help books—will transform me into the image of Christ. Your kingdom principles are easy to understand but sometimes harder to put into practice consistently. Give me a determined heart to enter Your transformation program.*

## RUN TO ME

*R*UN TO ME. When you feel discouraged, run to Me. When you feel frustrated, run to Me. When you feel like you can't take another step, run to Me. When you feel like Father is not hearing your prayers, run to Me. When you don't feel My peace, My joy, My love, and My presence, know that I am still with you. Turn to Me. Run to Me. Don't hesitate. Don't delay. Don't try to do this in your own strength. Run to Me. You will find Me.

PSALM 31:1; PSALM 119:32; PSALM 141:8

### ⟶ PRAYER ⟵

*Remind me to run to You in the heat of the moment when there is pressure mounting against my mind. Remind me to run to You amid the battle when I am tempted to lay down my weapons. Remind me to run to You for anything and everything. I need You.*

*August 30*

## You Can Grow From Your Mistakes

Mistakes are a part of life, a part of growth. Father would never rebuke you for making an honest mistake. Practicing sin is what grieves His heart and Mine. Set your mind and soul to learn from your mistakes, and you will be less likely to repeat them. Be determined to learn and grow from your missteps, and you will. Be ready and willing to see things in a new way, and I will show you how you can avoid repeating the same mistakes over and again.

Proverbs 1:5; Proverbs 9:9; Proverbs 1:7

### ⊹ Prayer ⊹

*I am ready, and I am willing. I am grateful there is no fear in love, because fear brings torment. You are a faithful Teacher, and You want to see me thrive. Help me learn from the mistakes I make. Show me what I could have done and should have done.*

## Never Fear Anything, Ever

WHEN IT COMES to fear, the key word is *never*. Never fear. Never let circumstances move you. Never let the devil see you sweat. Never let people intimidate you. Never forget that all of heaven is for you. Father did not give you a spirit of fear but of power, love, and a sound mind. If I am for you, then who can be against you? Never fear even fear itself. It's under your feet.

ISAIAH 41:10; 2 TIMOTHY 1:7; PSALM 34:4

### ❖ PRAYER ❖

*Your words strengthen my heart. Thank You for assuring me that I have nothing to fear. I am confident in You. Help me to root out any hidden fears from my heart. Help me stand strong in the face of adverse circumstances. Teach me to walk in power, love, and a sound mind.*

# September

*Blessed is the man who walks not in the counsel of the ungodly, nor stands in the path of sinners, nor sits in the seat of scoffers; but his delight is in the law of the LORD, and in His law he meditates day and night. He will be like a tree planted by the rivers of water, that brings forth its fruit in its season; its leaf will not wither, and whatever he does will prosper.*

—PSALM 1:1–3

## YIELD TO GODLY PRESSURE

SOMETIMES THE ONLY way out is through. Sometimes the only way through is a narrow path that puts pressure on your flesh and your very personality. If you yield to it, that pressure will prune away bad fruit in your soul. That pressure will encourage you to die to your wants, your unnecessary needs, your ungodly desires, and your very self. Yield to the pressure. Choose the narrow path that produces more freedom in your soul and more victory in your life.

1 CORINTHIANS 10:13; PSALM 118:5–6;
1 PETER 1:6–7

### ✦ PRAYER ✦

*I will choose the narrow path, but I don't enjoy the pressure. Help me to appreciate the process. Show me how to yield so that I am not pressing back against Father's will. Teach me how to willfully let go of the attitudes, emotions, and habits that are holding me back.*

## September 2

### A NEXT-LEVEL LIFE AWAITS YOU

*A* GREATER LEVEL OF peace awaits you. A greater joy beckons you. A greater faith is ahead of you. A greater glory is in store for you. Greater things are coming your way. Ask for them. Expect them. Wait earnestly for them. Desire them. Supernatural peace and joy belong to you. You are growing from faith to faith, and I am changing you from glory to glory. Stay close to Me. Listen for my voice. Heed my direction. Exciting days are ahead.

2 THESSALONIANS 3:16; JOHN 16:33; ISAIAH 26:3

### ✦ PRAYER ✦

*Give me the greater things! Let me do the greater works. Help me stay focused on the next level so I don't stumble and fall over my own plans. Teach me to listen fully and completely before I begin racing toward the greater glory. Remind me that apart from Christ I can do nothing.*

## LISTEN MORE THAN YOU SPEAK

*L*ISTEN TO PEOPLE when they speak. Listen more than you speak and you will learn much. You already know what you know. You will not increase in knowledge by talking. You will increase in knowledge by hearing. Be quick to hear and slow to speak, weighing your words for maximum impact. Avoid speaking and listening to idle chatter that can turn into gossip. Speak words of life and listen closely. These are wise words that will take you far if you receive them.

JAMES 1:19; PSALM 141:3; PROVERBS 18:13

### ✦ PRAYER ✦

*Such wise counsel. Please help me to heed Your words. Please alert me—give me a check in my spirit—if I am about to open my mouth when I should be inclining my ears. Give me ears intent on learning so that I can grow. Give me a mouth intent on speaking words of life.*

## September 4

## I Am Calling You Upward

*U*PWARD IS WHERE I am calling you. Upward is where I want to take you—up, up, and away from your current challenges and into a broad place of promotion. Remember you are actually already seated in heavenly places in Christ Jesus. You are already far above all principalities and powers. The enemy is already under your feet. I am calling you upward in the revelation of these realities so you can see clearly where you truly stand.

PHILIPPIANS 3:14; ISAIAH 54:2;
EPHESIANS 1:20–21

### ✦ PRAYER ✦

*Your words are empowering. They are light
and life to my soul. I say yes to Your call to
go higher and to step into the broad place.
What do I need to let go of in order to answer
this call? What is holding me back from
the next phase of my journey with You?*

## DON'T WASTE YOUR TRIALS

*D*ON'T WASTE YOUR trials. Don't waste your pain. Don't waste any life experience, whether good or bad. There are lessons in the storm. There are treasures in the trials. There is wisdom hidden in the times of testing and seasons of tribulation. Don't just look for a way of escape from the drama. Look for My presence. Look for My hand at work. Look for My heart for you. Look for the lessons to learn. You will discover truths from searching like this that will help you get around the next mountain.

ROMANS 5:3–5; JAMES 1:2–4; JAMES 1:12

### ✦ PRAYER ✦

*Jesus never wastes anything—not even the few loaves and fishes He used when He fed those many thousands of people. Show me what I need to see when I encounter fiery trials and painful situations. Show me the takeaways that will help me walk away wiser.*

## September 6

### LOVE ALL PEOPLE

*T*HERE WILL ALWAYS be people you won't get along with as well as you do with others. You will connect with certain ones faster than others. Your past experiences with people and places have helped to shape who you are and what you like and dislike. That being true, love all people and don't immediately write someone off just because you aren't clicking with him right away. Some people you don't initially like may be among your best friends in the future.

PROVERBS 18:24; PROVERBS 17:17;
PROVERBS 27:17

### → PRAYER ←

*Holy Spirit, help me pick my friends. At times, I've chosen the wrong friends and caused myself great grief. I have probably overlooked a few gems over the years due to my first impressions of them. Please show me whom You want me to connect with in the days ahead.*

## YOUR SECRET WEAPON
## AGAINST TEMPTATION

SELF-CONTROL IS PART of My fruit, so exercise it. You have the seed of this fruit on the inside of you, so water it. Let it grow day by day, and you will discover that it will become easier and easier to resist the temptations of the enemy and the lusts of the flesh. Water that seed, and you will see discipline rise within you so that you can stay on the course that leads you to victory, where dreams come true.

GALATIANS 5:22–23; PROVERBS 25:28;
2 PETER 1:5–7

### → PRAYER ←

*I love this secret weapon. You have given me this gift of self-control. You have given me the ability to put down my flesh and follow Your will. You have given me directions and a blueprint for victory. Help me accept Your plans for my life.*

*September 8*

## YOU ARE SET APART

*I*T'S EASY TO go with the flow. It's simple to take the path of least resistance. But I haven't called you to go with the flow. I haven't called you to maintain the status quo. Yes, there will be times when I will lead you beside still waters, and yes, My grace is sufficient so that even impossible things are possible to you. But you are set apart. You are called. You are chosen. When you follow Me on the path marked by resistance, I will strengthen you along the way.

MATTHEW 10:14; MATTHEW 10:28;
DEUTERONOMY 31:6

### ⇢ PRAYER ⇠

*I've never been one to go with the flow, but the resistance is real. The opposition is fierce at times. The pushback is great. Still, You are stronger and greater and higher than any resistance. Give me a determined heart to press through every challenge.*

## COMMIT TO BEING A LOVER
## OF THE TRUTH

*L*OVE THE TRUTH. Seek the truth. Believe the truth. Obey the truth. The truth will renew your mind. The truth will keep you free from the deceptive seeds the wicked one tries to plant in your mind about you, other people, or even Me. The truth will serve to light the pathway to your destiny. The truth will guard you and keep you in any circumstance. Jesus is the Truth. Love Him. Seek Him. Believe Him. Obey Him.

2 THESSALONIANS 2:10; LUKE 8:50; JOHN 14:15

### → PRAYER ←

*I want to be a lover of the truth. I want to see You all my days. I want to believe and walk in Your Word. Show me any area of my mind that is vulnerable to doubt or disobedience. Show me where I need to renew my mind with Your glorious truth.*

## September 10

### I Will Show You What You Need to See

Sometimes I don't show you everything to come for your own good. Seeing it all may overwhelm you. It may cause you to enter into pride. It may frighten you. It may cause you to try to push open doors or run too fast to the place I have prepared for you. It may cause unnecessary warfare against your life. It may have many ill effects on your soul. Even though I don't always show you everything to come, I will always show you what you need to see.

JEREMIAH 33:3; JOHN 16:13; PROVERBS 29:23

### ⤙ Prayer ⤚

*I don't need to see it all. I want to see only the things You want to show Me. Help me guard my heart from pride about what I think might happen or where I think You are taking me. Help me not to get ahead of You or open a door for the enemy's attack.*

## LEARN THIS LESSON NOW

*P*AIN CAN BE a great teacher, but I would rather teach you Myself. Pain can serve as a reminder not to repeat the same actions, but I'd rather teach you with Father's Word. There is enough trouble in this world and enough suffering in life. It grieves Me to watch you endure pain that you could have avoided. Learn this lesson now: ask Me before you make major decisions. Come to Me for advice about your plans. I can help you avoid the pain.

PROVERBS 12:15; PROVERBS 16; 1 KINGS 12:6–19

### ✦ PRAYER ✦

*I've had enough pain in my life. I've made enough mistakes. Please help me remember to seek Your counsel before I move ahead. Help me not to act in haste or make rash decisions. Help me use wisdom in my words and my actions.*

## I Will Reveal Hidden Mysteries to You

*B*EFORE THE WORLD was, I was. Before you were, I was. I am eternal, and because you believe in the Son, you will have eternal life. Consider this for a moment: eternity with your Savior; eternity with the risen Christ; eternity with your Father who loves you; eternity with Me. In the ages to come, you will continue gaining wisdom, knowledge, and understanding about the kingdom. As you do, your love for Us will grow greater and greater, and you will come to understand hidden mysteries.

REVELATION 22:13; JOHN 3:16; JOHN 17:3

### ⋆ PRAYER ⋆

*You are the Eternal One, and I worship and adore You. Thank You for rescuing me out of the kingdom of darkness and translating me into the kingdom of light. Thank You for the promise of eternity with the everlasting God who loves me completely. Help me grasp eternal realities.*

## HEALING BELONGS TO YOU

*H*EALING BELONGS TO you. Jesus paid the price for your healing. Sickness and disease have no authority to come near your dwelling place—unless you allow them. Stand against infirmity like you would stand against a bully because that's what it is. Sickness and disease try to scare you into accepting their lies. Stand strong against them, and battle for the divine health that belongs to you.

JEREMIAH 17:14; JEREMIAH 33:6; PSALM 41:3

### ⇥ PRAYER ⇤

*I refuse to bow to sickness and disease. I reject
every infirmity. I stand strong in the power
of Your might against ailments and injuries.
Show me the subtle ways the enemy tries to
rob my health. Teach me how to walk in the
divine health Father has ordained for me.*

## September 14

### Father Hears Your Desperate Cries

You don't have to beg Father to give you good gifts. He's Father, and you are His favorite one. You don't have to plead for Father to answer your petitions as if you are asking them of an unjust judge. Father will provide what you really need when you ask. He knows what you need before you ask. Desperate prayers rooted in complete trust in Him will not be ignored. He hears you.

Matthew 7:11; Matthew 6:8; Psalm 142

### → Prayer ←

*I am always desperate, but I know there's a difference between desperate prayer in faith and double-minded begging. Help me to posture my heart with confidence before You. Help me to bring my petitions before Father's throne with the right measure of boldness and humility.*

## REJECT THE CARES OF THIS WORLD

*J*ESUS LAID IT all down for you. What are you willing to lay down for Him? How about starting with the cares of the world, the doubts and fears that try to move you away from His heart, and the striving? When you lay down the things He didn't give you, you will more easily enter His rest. Lay them down. Cast them on Him. He can handle it.

MARK 4:19; JAMES 1:6; EXODUS 33:14

### ✦ PRAYER ✦

*I am willing to lay everything down for the One who saved me—even my very life. How gracious You are to invite me to lay down those things that hinder my race. Please show me how to let go of these things once and for all so I can run swiftly.*

## September 16

### TAKE A FREE-FALL INTO MY LOVE

*P*EOPLE SPEAK OF falling in love. What if
you just took a free-fall in My love? What
if you just totally let go and trusted Me to catch
you? What if you used your faith to receive more
of My love, more of My heart for you, more of My
truth, more of Me? We're on this journey. Fall into
Me. Fall into love. I will catch you and take you on
a wonderful adventure.

EPHESIANS 2:8–9; PROVERBS 3:5–6;
1 CORINTHIANS 2:5

### ✦ PRAYER ✦

*Oh, how You love me, and oh, how I
love You. I will free-fall into Your loving
arms. Thank You for being so trustworthy.
Thank You for always catching me. Help
me to totally surrender my heart to You
and follow You on this divine adventure.*

## DECIDE TO LIVE IN JOY

*Y*OU HAVE FREE will. You can decide. So choose to walk in love. Decide to live in the joy of the Lord. Pick peace. Surround yourself with people who do the same, people who edify you and love you back. If you don't like what is going on in your life, change it. You have choices. Choose to frame your life with My love.

ROMANS 15:13; GALATIANS 5:22; PSALM 16:11

### ✦ PRAYER ✦

*So much of life comes down to my own decisions. You've already given me everything I need to live in victory, peace, joy, and love. Teach me how to tap into the life-changing power You offer. Show me how to walk in what is available to me.*

*September 18*

## THINK ABOUT WHAT COULD GO RIGHT

*E*VERYTHING IS GOING to be OK. Just keep following Me. Don't go somewhere in your mind that will never be a reality. Don't think about what could go wrong. Think about what could go right. Think about the outcome you want to see, and ask Me to bring it pass—or something better. I am with you in this. I have a plan. Just keep following Me. I will lead you into a broad place.

PHILIPPIANS 4:8; ROMANS 8:5–6; COLOSSIANS 3:2

### ⤜ PRAYER ⤛

*My mind does work overtime to figure things out. Help me trade excessive reasoning for Your wisdom. Help me set my mind on what is pure, lovely, and of a good report instead of considering the worrisome thoughts that plague my mind. Teach me to follow You.*

# Give Honor to Whom Honor Is Due

*P*UTTING OTHERS FIRST is not always easy. Your flesh cries out for its own way. But Jesus says to prefer others. Dying to your own preferences can cause a war in your soul. Sacrificing your own needs for another's can even cause resentment if you don't guard you heart. Set boundaries, but honor and walk in love with those around you. Love is the principal thing.

ROMANS 12:9–13; 1 PETER 2:17–18;
1 CORINTHIANS 13:4–8

## ✦ PRAYER ✦

*Honor is so rare in today's society, yet I want to be a person of honor. Teach me how to be truly honorable in every thought, action, and deed. Show me how to honor others rightly. Help me to honor others as unto the Lord.*

## September 20

### REMEMBER THE JOY OF YOUR SALVATION

REMEMBER THE JOY of your salvation. On those days when you feel downcast and worn out, on those days when you feel like everything is against you, remember the joy, love, and strength you experienced when you gave your heart to Jesus. Remember how the cares of the world lifted off your shoulders. Remember that unspeakable joy still belongs to you.

PSALM 51:12; ROMANS 15:13; 1 PETER 1:8

### ✦ PRAYER ✦

*I do remember the joy of my salvation. It was a new beginning. Help me to remember that feeling of being translated out of the kingdom of darkness and into the kingdom of light. Remind me of what belongs to me as a child of God, and I will praise You.*

## DECLARE THAT YOU ARE STRONG

W HEN YOU FEEL weak, declare that you are strong. Remember, I am your strength. You can do all things through Christ who strengthens you. My strength is made perfect—*perfect*—in your weakness. So instead of despising your weakness, rejoice in it because I am with you. Let the weak say, "I am strong." Again—let the weak say, "I am strong." Keep saying that until you feel My strength.

JOEL 3:10; PSALM 28:7; 2 CORINTHIANS 12:9

### → PRAYER ←

*I often feel weak, but I am grateful that Your strength is made perfect in my weakness. So I declare that I am strong in You and the power of Your might. I declare that I can do all things through Christ who strengthens me. And I rejoice in Your strength within me.*

*September 22*

## COMMUNICATE WHAT YOU NEED

*T*ELLING PEOPLE WHAT you prefer—or even what you don't like—is not a crime. It's not wrong to communicate what you want and need as long as you do it with a right spirit. In honor you should prefer one another, but when you are the only one bending in a relationship, then it's time to speak up. Many times people don't realize they are being inconsiderate. You need healthy boundaries.

GALATIANS 6:5; JAMES 4:1–2; EPHESIANS 4:26

### → PRAYER ←

*I realize we all have our own bag of troubles and that many people are selfish. Help me not to fall into self-centeredness, but show me how to take better care of myself. Teach me how to communicate appropriate needs and boundaries in a godly way.*

# I Am Giving You Grace and Wisdom

*I* love how you are so concerned about doing what is right by people, doing what is right in the marketplace, and otherwise doing what is right in My sight. Your quest for obedience thrills My heart. I am giving you grace, grace, and more grace, as well as wisdom upon wisdom to make the right decisions in every situation because you have shown yourself willing.

James 4:6; John 1:16; 2 Timothy 2:1

### → Prayer ←

*Obedience is my heart's desire. I know I will never reach a hundredfold obedience in thought, word, and deed while I'm walking this earth, but that is my goal. Strengthen me to obey. Lead me and guide me in obedience. Pour Your wisdom into my spirit.*

## STRIVE TO ENTER MY REST

*Y*ou need to get more rest. I don't mean physical rest. I mean spiritual rest. I want to see you not only enter My rest but also live, move, and have your being in My rest. I am faithful. It's part of who I am to stand by you and help you. So strive to enter My rest and determine to stay there. Labor to enter the true rest that belongs to you.

PSALM 127:2; PSALM 46:10; HEBREWS 4:11

### ✦ PRAYER ✦

*I know I need to learn to rest more completely in You. I am not resting when I am worrying or when I am upset. I am not resting when I am not trusting. Teach me how to enter Your rest. Show me the path of true spiritual rest that comes from faith in Christ.*

## I Am Your Power Source

*I* AM THE POWER source in Your life. Your flesh will carry you only so far. Your will can take you only so high. I am the power source in your life. Why would you rely on anything else to energize your body, refresh your soul, and strengthen your heart? I am the power source in your life. Depend, rely, and lean completely on Me, and you will not struggle. Stay close to Me, and you will not stumble.

ACTS 1:8; EPHESIANS 6:10; COLOSSIANS 1:11

### ✦ PRAYER ✦

*When I am struggling, I'm disconnected from Your power. Help me to discern quickly when I've moved beyond Your grace, when I am not leaning fully on Your strength, or when I am taking matters into my own hands and moving apart from You.*

## September 26

### I AM CONFIDENT IN YOU

*I* AM CONFIDENT IN you. I have more confidence in you than you have in Me. But that's OK. I will gain more and more of your confidence as you hear My voice, obey My instructions, and see the good fruit in your life. I am confident in this, and I am confident in you because I see your end from the beginning. It's a blessed end that never really ends at all. I look forward to a never-ending eternity with you.

PROVERBS 3:26; ISAIAH 41:10; HEBREWS 13:6

### ✦ PRAYER ✦

*You are so good and gracious and kind. You believe in me. Help me believe in You all the more. Teach me more about Your character so that my heart will be inspired to trust You more deeply. Show me ways You are working in my life that I haven't seen.*

## Walk by Faith and Not by Sight

*Y*ou don't need to know what something I'm bringing your way looks like, and you can't make decisions based on what that thing feels like. Many times what it sounds like brings worry and fear. Discern Me in a thing, and follow Me instead of what you feel and what you hear. I know where I am taking you, and I know what it looks like—and it's good. It's all good. Trust Me.

2 Corinthians 5:7; Psalm 37:5–6;
Jeremiah 29:11

### → Prayer ←

*Teach me how to walk by faith and not by sight, not by my emotions, and not by my own will. Teach me how to recognize Your promptings even when confusion is hitting my mind. Remind me not to make decisions with my natural eyes but by Your wisdom.*

## September 28

### You Can Do the Impossible

*I*F YOU FOLLOW ME, you can walk on water. If you follow Me, you can walk through fire. If you follow Me, you can raise the dead. If you follow Me—truly follow Me—you can do the impossible in Christ's name, by My power, and with Father's authority delegated to you in Christ. You'll have to stop following other things to follow Me at that level. How badly do you want it? Sanctify yourself to Me. I've called you to walk in miracles. Walk.

MATTHEW 14:22–31; MATTHEW 10:8;
1 CORINTHIANS 12:10

#### ✦ PRAYER ✦

*I will follow You—truly follow You—all the days
of my life, even though I realize I probably don't
fully understand what that means. Teach me how
to operate in supernatural realms. Show me how
to walk in the anointing that sets captives free.*

## I Will Give You Abundant Life

*I*F YOU DIE to self, you'll rise to life. True life. Life that's worth living. Life that makes lost souls hungry for what you carry. Life that never ends. Abundant life. Overflowing life. Life that breeds life. If you die to self, you'll rise with life—an empowered life that leads to victory over darkness, newness of life. I will exchange My life—*zōē* life, which is life eternal—for your life.

GALATIANS 2:20; PHILIPPIANS 3:8; LUKE 9:23

### ⇥ PRAYER ⇤

*What an offer. What a good God I serve.*
*I will crucify my flesh. I will pick up my*
*cross and follow Christ. I will die to self—*
*but I need Your all-sufficient grace to help*
*me follow through with my vow. Show me*
*the way to experience the life of God.*

284          *Evenings With the Holy Spirit*

*September 30*

## Draw Close to Me

WHEN YOU AREN'T satisfied, you're missing Me. When you aren't content, you're missing Me. When you are frustrated, you're missing Me. When you feel like something is missing, you're actually missing Me. Draw close to Me, and you will be satisfied, content, peaceful, and fulfilled. I am indeed all you will ever need. Look on Me.

JAMES 4:8; ISAIAH 55:1–3; PSALM 65:4

### ✦ PRAYER ✦

*Better is one day in Your courts than a thousand elsewhere. In Your presence is everything that I will ever need. Teach me how to practice Your presence. Show me how to dwell in that secret place as I move throughout my day. You are all I need.*

# October

For thus says the High and Lofty One who inhabits
eternity, whose name is Holy: I dwell in the high
and holy place and also with him who is of a contrite and humble spirit, to revive the spirit of the
humble, and to revive the heart of the contrite ones.

—ISAIAH 57:15

## The Best Is Yet to Come

*T*HE BEST REALLY is yet to come. You have seen only the firstfruits of My blessings on your life. You have not seen or even imagined My best for you. What has passed you by and passed you up looked good, but the better part is coming your way. Your eye has not seen nor has your ear heard, nor has it even entered into your heart what Father has prepared for you in His great love. The best is yet to come.

HAGGAI 2:9; JOB 8:7; 1 CORINTHIANS 2:9

### → PRAYER ←

*When I look back over my life, the evidence of Your goodness overwhelms me. Father saved me from the pit of hell by sacrificing His only begotten Son. I can't imagine what You have planned next, but help me to walk in the fullness of what my eyes have not yet seen.*

*October 2*

## I Am Waiting to Be Found

*I*F YOU PURSUE Me with your whole heart, you will not only find Me, but you will also see Me in a fresh way. You will see Me in a way that changes your perspective of the kingdom. You will see Me in a way that causes you to willingly walk away from everything that would hinder love. It won't be a struggle, and there will be no temptation to turn back. You'll be sold out to Father's will completely—if you pursue Me. I am waiting to be found by you.

MATTHEW 6:33; MATTHEW 22:37;
PROVERBS 23:26

### ✦ PRAYER ✦

*I am pursuing You. Help me find You. Show me Your kingdom, Your glory, and Your kind intentions toward me. Give me a glimpse of what I have not yet seen. Inspire my heart to give You the preeminence. Help me find You.*

## You Will See My Hand on Your Life

Opportunities. I have more opportunities prepared for you than you can ask, think of, or imagine. I have prepared you for opportunity. I am paving the way for opportunity. I am leading and guiding you into opportunity. All you have to do is yield to Me, listen for My voice, and reject the opportunities that are not in line with My will. You will see My hand on your life.

Ephesians 5:6; Revelation 3:8; Proverbs 8:34

### ✦ Prayer ✦

*You are a God of opportunities. You are a God of open doors. Would You help me discern which doors You want me to walk through? Would You show me which opportunities to turn down? Help me stay in Your perfect will.*

## I Love to Sing Over You

*I* LOVE IT WHEN you sing to Me. I love to hear you make a joyful noise. I love to hear you sing Father's praises and proclaim your adoration for Christ. I love to hear you sing psalms, hymns, and spiritual songs, and I love to sing over you with songs of deliverance that set you free from worries and cares and all manner of maladies attacking your mind.

PSALM 95:1–2; COLOSSIANS 3:16;
ZEPHANIAH 3:17

### → PRAYER ←

*I will sing of Your love forever. I will sing of*
*Your great grace forevermore. I will sing of*
*Your mercy and Your joy. I want to hear You*
*singing over me. Open my spiritual ears and*
*let me hear You singing over me with rejoicing.*
*Let me hear the melodies of Your heart.*

## Think About My Great Love for You

*Y*ou have no idea how much I love you. You really have no understanding of how deep, how wide, how long, and how high My love for you is. I love you with a perfect love. I love you with an *agape* love. I love you with all My heart, all My mind, all My soul, and all My strength. Think about that. Really think about that. Think about it often. Think about it when other thoughts try to suggest otherwise.

Ephesians 3:18–19; Romans 8:38–39;
1 John 4:10

### → Prayer ←

*Would You reveal Your heart to me in a deeper way? Would You show me the depths of Your love? Would You share with me what I can comprehend in this season and prepare my heart to receive more and more and more? Help me consider often Your great love for me.*

## I Am Your Faithful One

*I* AM YOUR SAFETY. I am your security. I am your peace. I am your resting place. I am your joy. I am your wisdom. I am your Faithful One. I will always be true to you. I will always advocate for you. I will always make intercession for you. I will always stand by you. I am always with you wherever you are and for whatever you need. Let me help you.

PSALM 4:8; PSALM 91; GALATIANS 5:22

### ✦ PRAYER ✦

*Indeed, You are my everything. Forgive me for overlooking Your presence. Forgive me for neglecting to turn to You in times of need. Help me to remember You are for me and that You are waiting patiently for me to turn to You for anything I lack.*

## Put Things Into My Perspective

*P*UT THINGS INTO perspective—put things into My perspective. Ask me to show you how I see a thing, what I think about it, and how it makes Me feel. Then you will understand the big picture. Then you will discern rightly what to say and do, and where to go and with whom to stand. Then you will align your soul with Me. Remember, we're in this together. Ask Me for guidance.

2 Corinthians 4:18; Isaiah 55:8; Romans 8:18

### ✦ Prayer ✦

*Show me how You see things, what You think about them, and how they make You feel. Help me to understand Your perspective on all matters of life—and about other people. Give me guidance in the affairs of life so I can walk worthy of my calling.*

## COME TO MY SECRET PLACE

*I* WANT TO SHOW you a hiding place. It's a special place in Me, a secret place. You will find it by seeking My face. You will discover it through studying Scripture. You will navigate your way there through prayer released in faith. And you can abide there. When you abide in Christ and He abides in you, your labor of love in the secret place will bear much fruit in your heart.

PSALM 119:114; PSALM 91:4; PSALM 27:5

### ⟶ PRAYER ⟵

*I want to go with You wherever You go. What a thrill it is for me to be invited by You into Your refuge, Your shelter, and Your hiding place. Help me navigate my way in the spirit, to pass through my flesh and my reasoning, so that I reach the secret place where Your Spirit dwells.*

## Don't Let Your Heart Grow Weary

*I* know you are tired, but don't grow weary. It's normal and natural to be tired—even exhausted. Jesus set Himself apart to pray and to rest, and He told His disciples to do the same. It's OK to rest. Just don't allow yourself to grow weary in doing good. There's a difference. Rest will cure your fatigue, but a weary heart is dangerous to your destiny. Ask Me for the spiritual strength you need to keep fighting the good fight of faith.

Galatians 6:9; Jeremiah 31:25; Isaiah 40:28

### ⤖ Prayer ⤙

*Thank You for the encouragement. I understand the difference and will guard my heart from weariness, especially in the mundane seasons of life. Would You show me when I am reaching a danger point and in need of rest so I can pull back and pray?*

## I Love You Just the Way You Are

*Y*ou are wanted. You are loved. You are greatly loved. See yourself in this light. You don't have to prove yourself to Me. You don't have to prove your love to Me. Just sit in My presence and fellowship with Me. Talk to Me and listen to Me. I will pour My love upon you, and you can pour My love out on others. I love you just the way you are.

Romans 8:38–39; Romans 5:8; Jeremiah 31:3

### ✦ Prayer ✦

*You have a way with words. You have a way of making me feel loved beyond measure. You listen to me when I pour out my heart, and You are always there to comfort me. Help me to receive more and more of Your unending love.*

## RECEIVE FATHER'S FORGIVENESS

ALL OF MANKIND falls short of Father's glory. He who says he has no sin is a liar. There's a difference between battling sin and practicing sin. When you think or say or do things outside Father's perfect will, there is a path to repentance. There is forgiveness. So repent when you miss the mark. Receive Father's forgiveness and keep fighting. Wallowing in guilt and condemnation will just wear you out.

ROMANS 3:23; HEBREWS 8:12; MICAH 7:18–19

### ✦ PRAYER ✦

*I'm grateful for the path to repentance. I'm grateful that Father is ready, willing, and able to forgive because of my faith in Jesus Christ. Help me to be quick to turn from the condemnation the enemy offers. Help me to learn to receive Father's forgiveness quickly and move on.*

*October 12*

## ACCEPT THIS DIVINE EXCHANGE

*I* DON'T KNOW WHY you choose to carry around those heavy burdens day in and day out. Your mind repeats the problems, and your imagination runs wild sometimes. You can choose right now to engage in that divine exchange. Give Jesus your burdens and take on His burdens. His burdens are light. Take the enemy's yoke off your neck and take on Christ's yoke, which is easy. Go ahead and do it now.

MATTHEW 11:28–29; PSALM 55:22; 1 PETER 5:6–7

### ✦ PRAYER ✦

*I refuse to be enslaved again to the enemy's yoke of bondage. I don't know why I insist on carrying my burdens when Jesus offered to carry them for me. Teach me to humble myself and ask You for the help I need. Help me to make this divine exchange You've offered me.*

## I AM SOVEREIGN

Sometimes coincidence is just coincidence. More often though, you don't discern how I am working on your behalf. You don't see how I am ordering your steps or notice the ways I am orchestrating everything according to the counsel of Father's will. And that's OK. Many times you might take matters into your own hands if you could see what I am doing. And I love to surprise you.

Daniel 4:35; Psalm 135:6; Romans 11:36

### ✦ PRAYER ✦

*I don't want to take matters into my own hands. Please help me rely on Your sovereignty. Please help me stand still when I should stand still and walk when I should walk. Surprise me with Your loving-kindness.*

## I Will Meet Your Every Need

Sometimes you think you need more rest, more revelation, or more alone time—or more of this or more of that. And sometimes you might. But what you always need is more of Me. Turn to Me first when you feel anything is missing or lacking. I will tell you what you really need in that moment. I will meet your every need if you will receive. Only receive.

2 Corinthians 9:8; Psalm 37:25–26;
Matthew 6:33

### ✦ Prayer ✦

*You're right. I think I know what I need, and I think I'm praying rightly, but many times I have no clue. I'm grateful that You know all things. Prompt me to turn to You when I am in need in any way. Pour out Your wisdom, grace, and love over my soul.*

## EXPECT PRAYER ANSWERS

Sometimes you are not getting the answers you want because you are not asking Me the right questions. Sometimes you don't know what questions to ask. Sometimes you ask the right questions but don't sit still long enough to hear the answer. So what are you supposed to do? Sometimes the blanket prayer for wisdom and revelation is best. But when you pray, expect the answer. Look for the answer.

MARK 11:24; MATTHEW 6:7; LUKE 18:1

### ⇥ PRAYER ⇤

*I don't want to pray amiss, yet sometimes I realize I don't know how to pray rightly. I don't know what I really need. Help me pray accurate prayers. Show me what to pray. Teach me to quiet my spirit long enough to hear Your voice. Give me wisdom and revelation concerning prayer.*

## October 16

### Ask Me for the Gift of Hunger

*H*unger is a gift. So ask Me for it. Those who hunger and thirst after righteousness shall be filled. Those who hunger after My presence will find satisfaction in Me. Those who hunger to move in My gifts will find opportunity to bring Jesus glory. Those who thirst for living water will find refreshing. Stay hungry. Stay thirsty. I will continue to meet you in that state.

Matthew 5:6; John 4:14; Psalm 42:1

### ✦ Prayer ✦

*Give me the gift of hunger. Let me find my comfort, my satisfaction, my joy, my peace, my acceptance, my everything in You. Help me stay hungry and thirsty for the Word and for Your presence. Teach me how to make others hungry for You.*

## STAY STEADY WITH ME

*I* DO NOT CHANGE. I will not change. I do not need to change. I am holy. I am good. I am kind. I am love. My heart is for you. My plans are for you. My thoughts toward you are steady. So stay steady with Me. Keep your mind stayed on Christ. Seek My presence. Choose to focus on Me, and you will discern Me. Keep steady. I do not change.

MALACHI 3:6; NUMBERS 23:19; JAMES 1:17

### ✦ PRAYER ✦

*I need to change. I need to be more like Jesus in my self-sacrifice. I need to be more like Father in my forgiveness. I need to be more like You in your grace. Please help me keep my focus on You so I can be transformed into Christ's image. Help me stay steady.*

## October 18

### WHAT WILL YOU CHOOSE?

THERE ARE MANY distractions day and night. There are many distractions working to keep you from seeking Father's face, from seeking My heart. You have a clear choice in front of you. You can choose to ignore the distractions and cry out to Me with everything in you, or you can remain less than fully satisfied. Choose to seek Me and you will find Me.

PSALM 25:12; JOB 34:4; JOSHUA 24:14–15

### → PRAYER ←

*You have set before me life and death. I choose life. I choose to put to death the enemy's distractions that try to take me off the course Father has set for me. I choose to dwell in Your presence despite the cares of this world or the distractions of people.*

## STAY ENCOURAGED WITH THIS TRUTH

*E*VERYTHING IS NOT always going to happen according to your best-laid plans. Things aren't always going to turn out the way you hoped they would. But don't let that discourage you. Find courage in the truth of Romans 8:28, which says, "We know that all things work together for good to those who love God, to those who are called according to His purpose." Love Father with everything in you. He can and will work it all out; He will turn it all around for your good when you trust Him. And He wants to.

JOSHUA 1:9; PSALM 31:24; PSALM 112:7

### ✦ PRAYER ✦

*Trust is the key word. I have confidence in You, and therefore I will be strong and courageous. I will not fear or be dismayed when bad news comes my way. Help me keep Your promises at the forefront of my mind. Teach me to encourage myself in the Word.*

## October 20

### I'M RIGHT BY YOUR SIDE

*I*'M STILL HERE. I'm right by your side. It seems you forget that sometimes. I hear your thoughts rolling over and over. You're getting nowhere in your mind. I hear your self-talk and your phone calls to friends about your problems. None of it takes you far from your concerns. Turn to Me. I'm still here. I never left your side. I'm here to help.

1 CORINTHIANS 3:16; REVELATION 3:20;
ROMANS 8:31

### → PRAYER ←

*I feel silly realizing that I so often search for counsel from people before I turn to You. Your Word promises me wisdom if I ask in faith, but sometimes the pressure pushes me to reason things out according to my own thoughts. Help me to lean on You with all that I am.*

## LISTEN TO MY HEART

*L*ISTEN TO MY heart and get ready for action. Sometimes I am calling you to sit with Me and learn of My ways. Sometimes I am calling you to walk with Me to new places that feel uncomfortable to your soul. Sometimes I am calling you to run with Me into a new dimension of your destiny. Discern when it's time to sit, walk, and run. Stay in My timing.

JAMES 2:17; JOHN 10:27–28: PSALM 25:4–5

### ✢ PRAYER ✢

*I am listening. I am waiting. I am trying to discern Your direction. Don't let me miss Your heart in the midst of the racing speed of life. Help me discern Your gentle leading and wise guidance every step along the way.*

*October 22*

## Forgiveness Is a Gift

Forgiveness is a gift that you both give and receive. You cannot give away something you do not have. So receive My forgiveness fully. Receive the mercy that I have for you continually. Receive the grace that is openly available to you—and then give it all away. There is an abundant supply of all these things in My kingdom.

Matthew 18:21–22; Luke 6:37;
Psalm 103:10–14

### → Prayer ←

*I know forgiveness is a command. If You can do it over and over, so can I. Teach me how to truly forgive quickly. Help me not to linger on offenses. Show me Your great grace, mercy, and love so I can extend it to those who wrong me.*

# I Will Never Ignore the Cries of Your Heart

$\mathcal{I}$f you ask Me to come, I will. If you ask Me for wisdom, I will supply it. If you ask Me for strength, I will pour it out upon you. If you ask Me for comfort, I will oblige you. If you ask Me anything according to Father's will, I will hear you and answer you as much as it depends on Me. I will never ignore the cries of your heart, though the answer may come differently from how you first imagined.

Proverbs 15:29; Matthew 7:7–8; Psalm 34:17

## ✦ Prayer ✦

*I am asking. I am knocking. I am seeking with all that is within me. I want to experience the fullness of Your wisdom, Your strength, Your comfort, and everything else You have to offer me. Help me not to hold on to preconceived notions about the ways you might manifest Your love.*

*October 24*

## ADVERSITY MAKES YOU STRONGER

ADVERSITY MAKES YOU stronger in the end. Trials perfect your patience and mold your character. So let the winds blow, knowing they are not powerful enough to move you off Father's promises if you hold on to the truth. The truth is a weapon in the midst of a storm. The truth will keep you free from the temptation to believe what you see with your eyes alone. Walk by faith and not by sight.

1 PETER 5:10; 2 CHRONICLES 15:7; PSALM 34:19

### → PRAYER ←

*Let the winds blow, but give me the strength to stand amid the winds. Reassure my heart of Father's promises when it appears the very opposite is happening in my life. Give me a determination to swing the sword of the Spirit in the midst of the battle.*

## Be Careful How You Hear

*Y*ou can believe what your Bible says, or you can believe what the enemy of your soul is whispering in your ear. You have a choice what you give your ear to, so be careful how you hear. Stop listening to the lies. Stop tolerating the attacks against your mind. Cast down imaginations. Take every thought captive to the obedience of Christ. You have the power and authority to do this. I won't do it for you.

Luke 8:18; 2 Timothy 3:16; Genesis 3:4–5

### ✦ Prayer ✦

*I believe the Bible. The Word of God is the final authority in my life. That crafty serpent comes suggesting that I am sometimes misunderstanding or misapplying Scripture. Help me rightly divide the Word of truth as I study to show myself approved. Help me catch the lies.*

## October 26

### You Can Make Me Feel Welcome

THERE ARE WAYS You can make me feel welcome in your home, in your car, in your church, or anywhere you go. When I feel welcome, I will abide in a place. I feel welcome where there is peace. I feel welcome where love is expressed. I feel welcome where Jesus is exalted. I feel welcome when I hear praises unto Father. I feel welcome when you talk about My goodness. I feel welcome when you ask for help and actually heed my counsel. You are welcome to come to me any time. You are always welcome.

PSALM 24:7; 1 JOHN 4:16; MATTHEW 5:8

### ✦ PRAYER ✦

*Thank You for teaching me how to attract Your presence. Although I know You are always with me, I also know that I can best sense Your presence where love, peace, and joy exist. Show me how to maintain an atmosphere where You feel welcome.*

## REJOICE IN THE MIDST OF ATTACKS

WHEN YOUR OLD enemies come around looking for that opportune time to strike, rejoice! That means you are making progress. When the tongue-waggers gossip and spread lies about you, rejoice. That means you are doing something right. When the devil uses people to attack you, rejoice and pray for those who curse you. You are blessed.

LUKE 4:13; MATTHEW 5:10; 1 PETER 4:14

### ❖ PRAYER ❖

*That is easier said than done, but I can do
all things through Christ who strengthens me.
Please strengthen me amid the gossip, slander,
and verbal persecution. Help me to stand
strong and wait for Father's vindication.*

*October 28*

## THIS IS JUST THE BEGINNING

*Y*OU'VE ONLY JUST begun. I know it seems like a long journey—and it is. It's an eternal journey that we are on together. But you haven't seen much yet. Your best days are ahead, both in this life on Earth and in life eternal. There is so much more. I have told you many times that your latter end will be greater than your past. I remind you of this truth so that you will take a long-term view. The best really is yet to come.

1 CORINTHIANS 2:9; 1 PETER 1:3;
ECCLESIASTES 3:11

### → PRAYER ←

*Life is long, and at the same time my life
on Earth is quick, just like the blink of an
eye. Help me to make the most of every single
moment. Help me to glorify Jesus so that on
that day in eternity I can hear Father say,
"Well done, My good and faithful servant."*

## ALWAYS SHOW COMPASSION

*I* DON'T JUDGE BY outward appearances, so you shouldn't either. You have no idea why some people act the way they do, so always show compassion. Love believes the best and suffers long. You don't know what motivates men's hearts, so don't make assumptions and presumptions about what drives people. When they behave poorly, pray for them and refuse to be offended. People are hurting and suffering from past traumas, and they don't need scrutiny; they need an encounter with Me. Pray for them.

LUKE 6:37; JOHN 7:24; JAMES 4:11–12

### ⇢ PRAYER ⇠

*Give me a heart that's sensitive to the hurts*
*and wounds of others. Help me see people*
*through Your eyes, not the eyes of judgment*
*and criticism. Teach me how to be an agent*
*of healing, and show me how to pray for those*
*who have been misunderstood and harmed.*

## Root Out Resentment

ESENTMENT IS A robber. Resentment will rob your peace of mind. Resentment will rob your creativity. Resentment will rob your time. Resentment is a thief that will rob your joy. Root resentment out of your heart. Don't ruminate on the past. Forgive yourself for allowing people to take advantage of you. Forgive them, and let go.

Ephesians 4:31; Hebrews 12:15;
Leviticus 19:18

### → Prayer ←

*I refuse to allow resentment to hold me
in bondage. I choose to let go of offenses
and forgive. I will not be seduced into
bitterness. I stand against all assignments
to bring me into spiritual slavery. I forgive
myself and those who have harmed me.*

## DON'T TAKE IT PERSONALLY

*W*HEN PEOPLE LET you down, break their word to you, or do something you've asked them over and over again not to do, don't take it personally. When you take it as a personal jab, your heart is more likely to become disappointed, offended, or resentful. Many people are thinking about themselves—what they need the most, and how to get it. Don't take their actions personally.

PROVERBS 19:11; ECCLESIASTES 7:21–22;
LUKE 17:3–4

### ✦ PRAYER ✦

*Father, I am grateful that You will never let me down. I am thankful that You are not a man that You should lie, nor the son of man that you should repent. Help me to adjust my expectations of people because we've all fallen short of Your grace. Give me the grace not to take people's mistakes as a personal assault.*

# November

*Enter into His gates with thanksgiving, and into His
courts with praise; be thankful to Him, and bless
His name. For the Lord is good; His mercy endures
forever, and His faithfulness to all generations.*

—Psalm 100:4–5

## Walk in Love With Yourself

**W**ALK IN LOVE, and keep healthy boundaries while you walk. These two things do not contradict each other. No, they work together. You need to walk in love with yourself, and if your boundaries are so low that you are worn out, then you won't love others well. Walk in love, but keep healthy boundaries.

MATTHEW 5:7; LUKE 5:16; MATTHEW 6:6

### ⊹ PRAYER ⊹

*I have never heard it explained in such a way—to walk in love with myself. Help me to receive Your love so that I can love myself in a healthy way. Teach me to set proper boundaries that allow time for my needs. Show me how to say no without fear and with grace.*

## Choose Not to Be Distracted

Distractions don't have to distract you. Distractions will surely come to compete for your attention. Distractions have a time-stealing agenda that aims to set you back. But the reality is that you can choose not to be distracted. You can choose not to give your attention to the distraction—or to the one who is distracting you. You can choose to stay focused. Deny distractions their power over you.

Psalm 119:15; 1 Corinthians 7:35;
1 Corinthians 10:13

### → Prayer ←

*Distractions are a constant issue—there are distractions from people, distractions from issues, and distractions in my own mind. Teach me how to stay focused on what really matters and shut the door on unnecessary distractions. Help me deny distractions.*

## You Are a King and Priest

*I* HAVE OWNERSHIP, BUT I've given you stewardship. Jesus is the King, but you are a king on the earth. Jesus is the Lord, but you are the lord in your realm of influence. Jesus is your High Priest, but you are a priest unto God. You have been created in His image and are being conformed into His image, faith to faith and glory to glory. You will be all He has called you to be. I will help make sure of it.

1 PETER 4:10; 1 PETER 2:9; ROMANS 8:29

### ⇥ PRAYER ⇤

*Father has made me a king and priest in Christ. What a privilege to rule and reign with Him. Help me yield to the process of changing from glory to glory as You transform me into His image. Teach me how to embrace the changes You are bringing into my life.*

## TURN TO ME FIRST

*I* AM MORE THAN you could ever need. I have more than you could ever want. I will do more in your life than you could ever possibly ask, think, or imagine. So look to Me first. Ask of Me first. Turn to Me first. Give Me first place in your thoughts, words, and actions. Consider Me in all things because I consider you always. I love you.

EPHESIANS 3:20; JOHN 15:15; PSALM 1:2

### ✦ PRAYER ✦

*You are more than enough—far more. I haven't yet begun to understand the depth of Your resources, Your grace, Your wisdom, or Your love. Help me to acknowledge You in all my ways. Teach me how to put You first in everything I think, say, and do.*

# I Will Put a New Song in Your Heart

*T*HERE IS INDEED a joy unspeakable and full of glory. Tapping into that joy and glory begins with intentional praise and purposeful worship. That doesn't mean sitting and singing songs all day. It means having a song in your heart. It means being aware of My joy in you and allowing it to shape your thoughts. Try it.

PSALM 40:3; JOHN 4:24; ROMANS 12:1

## ⤖ PRAYER ⤖

*You've given me a new perspective on praise and worship and on walking in Your presence. Thank You for showing me another way. Put a new song in my heart, and I will praise You all my days. Shape my thoughts, and help me walk in Your joy.*

*November 6*

## KEEP DECREEING, DECLARING, AND PRAYING

*T*HE ENEMY WILL always try to silence your voice. When you release My Word through your lips, when you share a word in due season, when you speak the truth in love, when you preach the gospel, when you decree and declare Father's will, when you pray without ceasing, you are a threat to the wicked one. Don't shrink back. Keep making noise about Jesus.

PROVERBS 25:11; EPHESIANS 4:15;
1 THESSALONIANS 5:16–18

### ⇥ PRAYER ⇤

*My heart will continually praise You. I will faithfully decree Your Word. Season my speech with grace. Compel me to preach Christ's gospel. Stir me to pray day and night. Inspire me to share my testimony with lost souls so that Jesus is magnified.*

## You Will Collect the Spoils of War

*B*E STRONG AND courageous. Be bold and fearless. Be ready and waiting. Be fierce and daring. When I lead you into battle, you need not fear or worry about the outcome. The outcome is guaranteed before you step on the battlefield. All you need to do is follow Me. Stick close to Me. Listen for My instructions, and you will collect the spoils of war.

JOSHUA 1:9; PROVERBS 28:1; 2 CORINTHIANS 2:14

### ✦ PRAYER ✦

*You assure me victory in every battle You lead*
*me into. Make me strong and fearless. Give*
*me courage and boldness. Prepare me for every*
*battle I must face. Lead me into triumph as*
*I seek to enforce Father's will on this earth.*

## Use These Two Keys to Victory

Repetition and consistency are keys to victory. It's not what you do once or even what you do every once in a while that will bring increase and change into your life. It's what you do with disciplined repetition and consistency that will drive the results we both want. I can help you stay steady. Lean on Me.

Hebrews 12:11; 1 Corinthians 9:27; 2 Peter 1:5–7

### ✦ Prayer ✦

*Help me to cultivate the fruit of virtue, knowledge, self-control, steadfastness, godliness, brotherly affection, and love in my life so I will not stumble. Help me stay steady on the path Father has ordained for me to walk upon.*

## I Want All of You

*I* GAVE YOU My life. I gave you My love. I gave you My gifts. I gave you My wisdom. I gave you My peace, joy, and more. What do I want in return, you ask? I want your life. I want your heart. I want your love. I will never ask you for more than you can give. I want all of you. Will you give Me you?

1 Timothy 6:13; 1 Timothy 6:17; Psalm 29:11

### ⤖ Prayer ⤛

*You have given me everything—and I did nothing to earn any of it. Your grace is matchless, and Your love is endless, so I give you all that I am and all that I have. I give you all of me. Help me to fully surrender.*

## November 10

### ASK ME FOR WISDOM DURING CONFLICT

*W*HEN YOU FIND yourself in conflict, think about how other people feel. Even when you are the one who was wronged, consider how the other person feels even if he reacts angrily. Even if people withdraw, consider that guilt and shame may be at work in them. Pride may be rising up in them. Consider how I feel about them, and ask Me how to respond when you find yourself amid conflict that seems to be growing.

PROVERBS 15:1; JAMES 4:1–2; EPHESIANS 4:26

### → PRAYER ←

*You are selfless. Help me to operate with this same mind. Teach me how to step into another's shoes and understand what he is thinking and feeling so I can respond with wisdom. Teach me how to live at peace with all men as much as it depends on me.*

## DON'T BRING YOUR YESTERDAY
## INTO TOMORROW

*T*OMORROW IS A new day. It's a new beginning. Don't bring your yesterday into tomorrow. I'm handling your yesterdays, and I'm handling your tomorrows. I'll even handle your today if you'll let Me. Try taking your hands off the matter and letting Me do what I do best: empower you, grace you, lead you, and guide you. Let Me teach you what to say and show you where to go. It's going to be a great day!

ECCLESIASTES 7:10; MATTHEW 6:34; LUKE 21:15

### ✦ PRAYER ✦

*I want You to handle everything—and give me the wisdom to make wise decisions. Teach me to let go when I need to let go. Tell me what to say when I have critical conversations. Show me where You want me to go tomorrow.*

## November 12

### LET ME MOVE YOU WITH COMPASSION

*L*ET ME MOVE you with compassion, and you may see miracles. Too many people are rushing along their daily routines without noticing the sick and hurting people around them. Too many are numb to the troubles of others. When Jesus was moved with compassion, miracles resulted. Stay sensitive to My heart, and let Me move you in the direction I want to take you. You could be an ingredient in someone's miracle if you yield to Me.

MARK 6:34; MATTHEW 14:14; COLOSSIANS 3:1–13

### ✦ PRAYER ✦

*Move me with compassion! Make my heart sensitive and pliable to You. Don't allow me to miss an opportunity to pray for someone who is sick or share a wise word with someone who is hurting. Help me see the needs of those around me.*

## STOP HOLDING GRUDGES
## AGAINST YOURSELF

*F*ORGIVE YOURSELF. STOP holding grudges against yourself. Quit thinking about what you could have done and what you should have done and what you didn't do. Let go of the guilt. When you asked Father for forgiveness, He granted it immediately. So why won't you accept it? Why are you still holding on to memories of things I long ago forgot?

JAMES 5:16; PSALM 103:10–14; ECCLESIASTES 7:20

### → PRAYER ←

*I am too hard on myself at times, but other times I don't realize that I am holding a grudge. Help me to fully receive Father's forgiveness and fully let go of any guilt or regrets I have about how I've handed people or issues.*

## FOCUS ON THE LONG-TERM

*W*HEN PEOPLE WANT to exit your life, don't try to hold on to them. Let them go if their minds are made up. Don't try to convince them to stay. Some are leaving because they never were supposed to be there at all. Others are missing Father's will, but you still have to let them go. I will always make it up to you. Focus on the long-term, and bless the out-goers.

1 JOHN 2:9; JOHN 6:54–68; LUKE 6:28

### → PRAYER ←

*I have seen people come, and I have seen*
*people go, but You are always with me.*
*Where can I go from Your Spirit? Where*
*can I flee from Your presence? Help me stay*
*focused on You and me. We are together in*
*this age and will be in the age to come.*

## WALK IN LOVE WITH THE UNLOVELY

*L*OVING PEOPLE WHO betray you may sound impossible and may seem impossible, but nothing is impossible in Christ. All things are possible to the one who believes. Believe Me for the grace you need to walk in love, even (and especially) when you would rather retaliate against them or curse them behind their backs. Choose to walk in love. It's really a choice.

MATTHEW 6:14–15; 1 CORINTHIANS 13:1–13;
1 PETER 4:8

### ✦ PRAYER ✦

*You amaze me. You are love; it's easy for You to love all people, no matter how they are treating You. I need to grow in love. I need to grow in grace. Please shed Your love abroad in my heart and help me choose love on all occasions.*

## DON'T WORRY ABOUT
## WHAT PEOPLE THINK

ON'T WORRY ABOUT or consider the potential consequences of what people are saying about you. People will always talk, gossip, and sometimes even slander. Don't compromise what you believe or how I have made you for fear of what people will think or say. It doesn't matter in the end—and it doesn't even matter right now unless you let it.

PROVERBS 29:25; MATTHEW 10:29;
GALATIANS 1:10

### ✦ PRAYER ✦

*Jesus made Himself of no reputation, and I will
do the same with Your help. Help me discern
when the fear of man is trying to creep into my
soul. Show me how to shut out the voices of gossip
or slander that rise up against me unjustly.*

## I Will Heal Your Wounds

*H*URT IS AN unfortunate but absolute reality of life. You won't advance in your kingdom assignment—whether it involves family, career, or ministry—without getting hurt from time to time. Some people will hurt you out of spite, and others will hurt you quite by accident. Either way, turn to Me, your comforter. Turn to Me, your counselor. I will wrap My love around you like a blanket and heal your wounds if you will let Me.

EXODUS 14:14; ROMANS 12:19; COLOSSIANS 3:13

### ✦ PRAYER ✦

*Processing hurt is not fun, but I realize it's a necessary part of life. Help me to be quick to forgive those who hurt me, whether knowingly or unknowingly. Teach me how to remain open and vulnerable, and how to avoid the temptation to put up walls.*

## I AM ON YOUR SIDE

S OME PEOPLE WILL stand with you until the end. Some people will say they will stand with you until the end but will walk away during a storm. There is a friend who sticks closer than a brother. There is One who will never leave you or forsake you. There is One who will never change His heart toward you. There is Father, Jesus, and Me. We are on your side.

MATTHEW 27:3–4; MATTHEW 24:10; PSALM 41:9

### ⟡ PRAYER ⟡

*All that matters in the end—and all that matters even now—is that You are standing with me. All of heaven is backing me. The angels are ministering on my behalf. Help me stay focused on these truths so I will not be moved when people move away from me.*

## I Am Thinking of You

As much as you think you need Me, you actually need Me much more. As much as you think I help you, I am actually helping you much more. And it's My pleasure. As much as you think of Me, I am actually thinking of you much more. My thoughts toward you are innumerable and good and lovely. You are My beloved one.

Psalm 139:17; Psalm 92:5; Psalm 144:3

### → Prayer ←

*It boggles my mind to consider how much
You think of me and how considerate You
are in all Your ways. Help me to be as
considerate of You and other people as You
are. Teach me how to grow in this area.
Share Your deep thoughts with me.*

## WHEN YOU'RE EXPERIENCING GROWTH PAINS

WHEN YOU FEEL as if you are off track with Me, don't get discouraged with yourself. Just get back on track. The fact that you discern you are off track indicates that you are sensitive to Me, for I am drawing you to My heart. Your life on Earth is a journey of growth and maturity in Christ. Sometimes you just experience growth pains as you enter a new phase of your life.

1 JOHN 1:9; REVELATION 3:19; ACTS 3:19

### ✦ PRAYER ✦

*You are so gracious. Thank You for letting me know when I get off track. Thank You for making me sensitive enough to You to discern your dealings. Let me always be quick to repent so that I can enter into refreshing.*

## REJECT YOUR REGRETS

$S$ITTING IN MY presence covered with guilt and battling regret will not enable you to make a joyful noise. Yet in My presence there is fullness of joy. So stop focusing on the past and reject the regrets. Seek forgiveness if you must, but shake off the thoughts and feelings that get in the way of enjoying My presence. It will be more enjoyable for both of us.

PHILIPPIANS 3:13–15; 2 CORINTHIANS 7:10;
PROVERBS 15:13

### ⟶ PRAYER ⟵

*I commit this day to reject guilt and to put
regret under my feet. They are destructive
forces that cannot stand in the face of
repentance and the blood of Jesus. Help
me to quickly move past these feelings
and embrace the fullness of Your love.*

## November 22

## WIELD THE WORD IN YOUR MOUTH

THE WORD IS alive! Declare it, confess it, wield it as a sword against the enemy, and let it convict your heart. Yield to the Word of God, and you will become more Christlike. Proclaim the Word in your home, in your business, and in your city, and watch things shift. Jesus gave you His authority to make decrees so that Father's will and Father's kingdom can manifest.

HEBREWS 4:12; 2 TIMOTHY 3:16–17; JEREMIAH 23:29

### ✦ PRAYER ✦

*I want to become more like my beautiful Savior each and every day. Therefore, I will confess His Word out of my mouth. I will meditate on Him. I will war with the sword of the Spirit. Give me the tenacity to keep pressing in.*

## I UNDERSTAND YOU

$\mathcal{S}$OME PEOPLE WILL misunderstand your words and deeds no matter how clearly you express yourself. Unless I tell you to, don't bother to offer explanations to someone who has already made up his mind about your motives. Give it to Me and march on, soldier! Remember that people misunderstood Jesus, so they will misunderstand you. But I understand you, and that's what matters most.

MARK 6:4; MARK 3:20–21; HEBREWS 2:18

### → PRAYER ←

*I hate being misunderstood or having the motives of my heart judged. Help me to respond rightly when the wrong thing is happening to me. Show me how to pray for a resolution instead of taking up for myself when someone is already convinced in his opinion about me.*

## CHOOSE YOUR WORDS WISELY

*B*EFORE YOU OPEN your mouth, consider your motives. If they aren't glorifying your heavenly Father, keep your mouth closed. Your words carry the power of death and life. You can bless, or you can curse. Be careful how you hear and what you say because you will give an account for every idle word on the Day of Judgment. Ask Me to help you tame your tongue and choose your words wisely.

PSALM 141:3; PSALM 19:14; PSALM 49:3

### ⸎ PRAYER ⸎

*Give me a greater revelation of the power of my words so that I will be responsible with every word I speak. Help me tame my tongue and choose my words wisely. Give me words of life to share with people. Let my speech build others up.*

## YOU ARE POISED FOR VICTORY

*B*E ENCOURAGED. I already saw that obstacle before you ran into it. Take a deep breath and pray. Father is still on the throne and working all things together according to the counsel of His will. Jesus is still sitting at His right hand making intercession for you. I am willing to pour out wisdom and strategies to help you break through. Be encouraged. You really can't lose if you just don't give up.

PROVERBS 24:16; MATTHEW 16:18; LUKE 10:19

### ✦ PRAYER ✦

*You see all things, and You know all things—
and You are faithful to lead and guide me
through all things. Thank You for Your wisdom.
Please show me how to get the breakthrough.
Teach me how to walk in total victory.*

## Enter Into Father's Blessing

You can't even imagine what Father has waiting for you—if you'll just obey. Don't look at your situation with natural eyes. See through My eyes, and the fear that's trying to convince you that you cannot and will not walk in Christ's promises will leave. The fear of embracing God's perfect will shall vanish. Then enter into His blessing. It's waiting for you.

Proverbs 16:9; Ephesians 2:10; Proverbs 19:21

### ⚜ Prayer ⚜

*Father has given me all things pertaining to life and godliness. I am blessed with every spiritual blessing. Yet I know that I lack the full revelation of this and much more. Help me to see my life through Your eyes. Show me how to receive His promises.*

## FATHER DELIGHTS IN YOUR
## PERSEVERING PRAYERS

THERE IS A fullness of time. Father is never slack concerning His promises. He has heard your persistent cries and is orchestrating plans for your life even now. He is always on time with prayer answers. Just be patient and know that He is preparing a table for you in the presence of your enemies. And He delights in your perseverance.

2 PETER 3:9; HEBREWS 6:12; PROVERBS 15:8

### ✦ PRAYER ✦

*I am grateful for the continual assurance
that Father hears my prayers. I know if
He hears me, He'll answer me and find a
way to deliver on His promises even when
things look dark. Give me the grace to
stand while I wait. Help me to persevere.*

## LET HOPE ANCHOR YOUR SOUL

EMOTIONS WILL BETRAY you if you let them. Keep your mind fixed on things above, and you'll avoid much of the turbulence in your soul. Consider the ways of your heavenly Father. Consider the sacrifice Christ made on Calvary. Consider the eternal life that belongs to you. Let hope anchor your soul, and reject emotions that torment your mind.

PROVERBS 15:13; JOHN 3:16; HEBREWS 6:19

### ✦ PRAYER ✦

*Emotions are fickle, but You are steady. Teach me how to put my emotions under the authority of Christ. Show me how to combat the emotions that rise up to defy Father's Word. I align My will with Your will and determine to press past contrary emotions.*

## PRESS INTO FATHER'S HEART

*E*VEN IF YOUR worst fear is true—and it's absolutely not—there's no sense in meditating on that fear. Press into Father's heart, and believe Him for whatever you need to get through this season. Father has given you power, love, and a sound mind to combat fearful thoughts. He's still on the throne, and He still loves you. Nothing has changed.

2 TIMOTHY 1:7; MATTHEW 14:27; PSALM 3:6

### → PRAYER ←

*Fearful imaginations do come, but I am committed to casting them down. The lies of the enemy have no place in my heart because my heart is filled with the love of God. Thank You that You have given me power over all the power of the enemy.*

## THE WAY TO VICTORY IS STRAIGHT AHEAD

*Y*OUR PAST IS in the past. I know that sounds obvious, but sometimes you don't act like you understand that. Your past only has the power over you that you give it. Don't let your past hold you down or hold you back. The only way through to total victory is straight ahead. Dwelling on the past only paralyzes you. Dwell on Jesus instead.

PSALM 56:3; PSALM 23:4; PSALM 91:3

### → PRAYER ←

*The past is the past, and Your future for me is bright, so help me immediately to reject emotions, thoughts, ideas, or any other marker from my past that would hold me back from the hopeful future Father has planned for me. I am pressing on!*

# December

*But our citizenship is in heaven, from where*
*also we await for our Savior, the Lord Jesus*
*Christ, who will transform our body of humili-*
*ation, so that it may be conformed to His glo-*
*rious body, according to the working of His*
*power even to subdue all things to Himself.*

—Philippians 3:20–21

## Trust Me in and Through Every Season

WHEN YOU'RE GOING through a season when you just don't understand what's happening, you can allow confusion, fear, and discouragement to strike your heart, or you can choose the better way. Decide in your heart to trust Me in and through every season. Make this decision while you are on the mountaintop, and it will be easier to stick to your convictions when you are in the valley. Father is trustworthy in every season of life.

PSALM 23:4; ISAIAH 43:2; PSALM 37:5

### ✦ PRAYER ✦

*I don't need to know all the answers because I know the One who does. I decide this day to trust You in the valley, through the storms, through the fire, and through everything else. Strengthen my resolve to stand on the Word in every season.*

## December 2

### BE CONFIDENT THAT I AM LEADING YOU

*T*HE CHAOS IN the world around you does not have to be on the inside of you. You can choose to walk in peace. The second-guessing that tries to come against your mind when you have a difficult decision to make doesn't belong to you. You can be confident that I am leading and guiding you. The weariness that tries to get you to quit has no power over you. Stand strong in Christ.

JAMES 1:6; MATTHEW 21:21; PSALM 143:10

#### ✦ PRAYER ✦

*Father has given me the measure of faith to choose life, peace, joy, strength, and whatever is needed in the moment. Help me discern the subtle voice of doubt that leads me into unbelief. Teach me how to combat weariness against my soul.*

## I Am Faithful

*H*AVEN'T I BROUGHT you this far? Haven't I delivered you from the enemy's hand every time he has attacked? Haven't I shown up for you in times of trial? Haven't I answered the cries of your heart in the midnight hour? Haven't I covered you and supplied you with the grace to walk out what I have spoken to your heart? I am faithful, and I delight in you. Let's keep walking this out.

2 TIMOTHY 2:13; DEUTERONOMY 7:9;
2 THESSALONIANS 3:3

### → PRAYER ←

*You are faithful, and You have proven that to me over and over again. I should never doubt You. Help my unbelief. Help me stand firm in my faith when everything looks like it is going to blow up. Help me walk closely with You every step of every day.*

## December 4

### I Will Share Father's Heart With You

F ONLY YOU could hear Father's thoughts toward you. So often and so clearly you hear what your critics say and what the enemy of your soul is saying. So often you get caught up in your own negative self-talk. But shut all that out and listen to My voice. Father's thoughts about you and toward you are good, kind, and lovely. Listen to My voice. I will share His thoughts with you.

JEREMIAH 29:11; PSALM 139:17; PSALM 40:5

### ✦ PRAYER ✦

*I know Father's thoughts toward me are good—they are innumerable. He even collects My tears in a bottle. Would you share with me His thoughts about me so I can gain a greater glimpse into His heart? Will You tell me what He thinks about my plans?*

## All I Want From You Is Your Love

*A*LL I WANT from you is your love. If you love me, you will obey Father. When you stumble, just repent. You have a beautiful Savior who loves you with a passion, and Father has sent Me to shed His love abroad in your heart so that you can love Him with all your heart, all your soul, all your mind, and all your strength. When you love that way, then obeying will not be a task. It will be a joy.

ACTS 5:29; 1 PETER 1:14; 1 JOHN 5:3

### ✦ PRAYER ✦

*You are kind and generous. Father saved me by sacrificing His only begotten Son, and Your power raised Him from the dead so that I could have eternal life. I owe You everything, yet all You want is my love. Give me an anointing to love You more.*

## December 6

### FOCUS YOUR HEART ON MY HEART

WHEN YOU ARE aware of My presence, you will find the strength you need in any situation. When you discern Me, you will have the words to speak at the right time. When you intentionally focus your heart on My heart, you will hear My voice louder than any other voice that may be speaking at the moment. Practice My presence.

PSALM 27:8; PSALM 145:18; PSALM 65:4

### ⇝ PRAYER ⇜

*There is nothing more important to me than Your presence. Make me more aware of Your presence. Teach me to discern You above all other influences. Help me to tune in to Your still, small voice. Teach me to focus my heart on Your heart.*

## THERE IS FREEDOM IN RECONCILIATION

*R*ECONCILIATION IS FREEING. Yes, there is freedom in reconciliation and joy in the restoration of relationships that the enemy came to destroy with false accusations. There is joy in the restoration of relationships that misunderstanding found a way into. Forgiveness and humility can pave the way to restored relationships that are stronger than before the attack. Pursue reconciliation and the freedom that comes with it.

ROMANS 12:18; 2 CORINTHIANS 5:18;
HEBREWS 12:15

### → PRAYER ←

*Father's Word commands me to live at peace with all men as much as it depends on me, and I have been given the ministry of reconciliation. Help me to forgive, and help those I've wronged to forgive me. Teach me to be a peacemaker so I can walk in Your blessing.*

## *December 8*

## I Love to Hear You Talk About Jesus

*I*LOVE TO HEAR you talk about Jesus and what He did for you at Calvary. My heart is to see Christ exalted in every area of your life. I love to hear you talk about the goodness of your Father in heaven. He records those conversations in His book of remembrance. I love when you talk about Me to your friends—and I love when you talk to Me. I am listening.

PHILIPPIANS 2:11; HEBREWS 12:2; MALACHI 3:16

### ⟶ PRAYER ⟵

*You are always listening to every word I say. Surround me with friends—and lost ones—who need to hear about Father's heart, Christ's great love, and Your very present help. Teach me to represent You rightly in my speech and my actions.*

## SEARCH MY THOUGHTS

*M*Y THOUGHTS ARE higher than your thoughts, but that doesn't mean you can't search them out. Search My heart, and you will find thoughts deeper and higher than your own. My thoughts will renew your mind with revelation and open your eyes to the principles of the kingdom. Search My thoughts, and you will understand more about My ways. Seek My thoughts, and you will find them.

PROVERBS 25:2; MATTHEW 7:8; PROVERBS 8:17

### ⚜ PRAYER ⚜

*What an invitation! What a promise! Give me the diligence to seek You and search out the treasures in Father's Word. Pour out a spirit of wisdom and revelation in the knowledge of the Word. Help me to find new dimensions of Your love.*

## December 10

### THE WORD NEVER FADES AWAY

*A*T THE END of the day—and at the end of this age—only faith, hope, and love will remain. So many things you rely on and put your confidence in will fade away. You are like a flower in the field, like a vapor, but I never change. The Word never fades away. Faith, hope, and love abide. Let them motivate your heart and drive your thoughts, words, and deeds. You will be greatly rewarded.

1 CORINTHIANS 13:13; PSALM 103:5;
MATTHEW 24:35

### → PRAYER ←

*Your commandments are not burdensome. They are liberating. Help me anchor my life in the Word. Give me the grace to do all that the Word commands. Help me align every thought, word, and deed with Scripture's instructions.*

## PURSUE PEACE WITH ALL PEOPLE

*P*URSUE PEACE WITH all people as much as it depends on you, and you will be blessed for your obedience. Do not let hurts and differences linger in your heart. Be quick to forgive. Be quick to repent. Be quick to hear a person out—and really listen. Be quick to reconcile with those who are truly willing to walk in peace.

PSALM 34:14; HEBREWS 12:14; ROMANS 14:19

### ✦ PRAYER ✦

*If I have unknown unforgiveness in my heart, please reveal it to me so that I can obey Christ's command to forgive. If there are hurts and wounds in my heart, please help me face these issues so I can receive healing. Teach me to pursue peace.*

## December 12

### YOU ARE THE APPLE OF MY EYE

*N*ow that I have your full attention, now that you have set your heart to hear My voice, I have something to share with you. You are the apple of My eye. I love you through and through. I look forward each day to our time together, and I'm always ready to spend more time with you. You have full access to My heart, My counsel, and My joy. Let's spend more time together.

ZECHARIAH 2:8; PROVERBS 13:10; PROVERBS 24:6

### ✦ PRAYER ✦

*I long to spend more time with You. It seems so many people and things are competing with You for my attention. Help me prioritize. Teach me to make better use of my time so I have more to spend with You. Your love moves my heart.*

## Seek, and Keep On Seeking

*S*eek. In this season set your heart and your mind to seek Me. Seek My truth. Seek My gifts. Seek My fruit. Seek My heart for you. Seek My ways. Seek My paths. Seek My joy. Seek My peace. These things belong to you, and I give them to you freely when you choose to seek and keep on seeking. Seek Me, and you will find Me. Seek the kingdom, and all of the rest will be added to you.

Hebrews 11:6; Psalm 14:2; Proverbs 8:17

### ✢ Prayer ✦

*I hear You. I will seek You, Your ways, Your paths, and everything else You lead me to seek. Thank You for the assurance that I will find what I seek. Give me an enduring spirit that refuses to give up the hunt for all that You have offered me.*

## December 14

### CRY OUT FOR JUSTICE

*J* HATE INJUSTICE. I hate unbalanced scales. I hate when people take advantage of My friends. When unjust things happen to you, pray for justice. Press in like the widow with the unjust judge in Luke 18. Cry out for justice. Take actions in faith, but believe Father to serve up justice. Jesus is a just judge, and He's making intercession for you even now.

JEREMIAH 22:3–5; PSALM 43:1; PSALM 94:15–16

### ✦ PRAYER ✦

*I love that Father is a God of justice. I love that Christ is a just judge. I am crying out for justice even now. Repay what the enemy stole. Vindicate me from my enemies. Take vengeance on the wicked one who spews lies about Your love for me.*

## Settle the Battle Over Your Will

*W*HEN YOU ALIGN your will with My will, you become unstoppable. You have a free will. You can do whatsoever you will. When you decide to obey the Word, when you decide to put your faith in Father's plan, when you decide to shout down the doubts and follow Jesus, nothing shall by any means stop you. The battle is real, but when the battle over your will is settled, the outcome is victory.

JAMES 4:7; JOHN 10:10; ROMANS 8:37

### → PRAYER ←

*I align my will with Your will even now. I choose to walk in obedience to the Word. I am determined to walk in faith. Please give me the grace of obedience. Help me to crucify my own will and carry my cross so I can see Your victory in my life.*

*December 16*

## WHAT DO YOU SEE WHEN
## YOU LOOK AT ME?

WHEN I LOOK at you, I see destiny. When I gaze upon you, I see the beauty of Christ's creation. When I think of you, I consider your love for Father. What do you see when you look at Me? I hope you see a friend who stands by your side, advocates for you, intercedes for you, strengthens you, and comforts you. This is who I am for you.

JOHN 16:7; ISAIAH 11:2; 2 CORINTHIANS 1:3

### ⟶ PRAYER ⟵

*I am a new creation in Christ, but I don't always see myself that way. The devil likes to remind me of my past, but You are showing me a future with eternal rewards. Help me see Christ as He really is so I can see myself rightly in Him.*

## PRAY MERCY ON THOSE
## WHO SOW DISCORD

ALSE ACCUSATIONS WILL come. Woe to those by whom they come. I hate when people bear false witness, and I hate a lying tongue. Beware of those who sow discord among brethren. Have no agreement with the works of darkness. Mark those who cause division among you. Forgive them of their trespasses, and pray for mercy on them. They are walking a dangerous road.

PROVERBS 19:5; PROVERBS 12:22;
PROVERBS 6:16–19

### ✦ PRAYER ✦

*Help me never to be on the accusing end of the equation. Set a guard over my mouth so I will not gossip or slander others. Help me to be a broker of peace. Defend me against lying tongues, and give me the grace of forgiveness so I can maintain my intimacy with You.*

*December 18*

## EXPECT FATHER TO MOVE ON YOUR BEHALF

FATHER HAS GIVEN you enough faith to see miracles in your midst, but sometimes you rely on the arm of the flesh to accomplish things. Sometimes you are depending on your own good works. Sometimes you are believing the lies of the enemy. Sometimes you are operating in unbelief because the problems seem too great. If you are going to strive, then strive to enter His rest. Expect Father to move on your behalf.

ROMANS 12:3; MATTHEW 17:20; HEBREWS 4:11

### → PRAYER ←

*Father is a miracle-working God. Jesus demonstrated what is possible—all things are possible. Would You help me build up my most holy faith? Would You root out any unbelief in my soul? Would You shine a light on the Word and give me revelation that will change my mind?*

## You Are Walking in My Favor

My light is shining upon you. You are walking in My favor. It's a season of favor like you've never known before. Embrace My favor by faith. Believe I am with you and that I will make connections for you that you could not possibly make on your own. Don't try to open doors. I will open them for you in this season of favor. Just walk through them with a determined heart.

Psalm 5:12; Psalm 90:7; Psalm 84:11

### → Prayer ←

*I'm so grateful that the favor of God rests upon my life. I'm thankful that You speak to the hearts of those who can help me fulfill Father's plan for my life. Please help me to understand, fully embrace, and walk in the favor that belongs to me as a child of God.*

*December 20*

## I Am Right Here With You

*M*ANY TIMES THINGS are exactly the opposite of what they appear to be. Many times the enemy shows you false evidence that appears real. Many times doubt and unbelief launch a one-two punch against your faith. When nothing looks right and everything is going wrong, remember I am right here with you and that you are the righteousness of God in Christ. Look at who I am and know who you are, and you will emerge victorious every time.

MARK 9:24; JOHN 14:1; ROMANS 10:17

### ✦ PRAYER ✦

*I know the devil has no power over me except what I give him. Father has given me power over all the power of the enemy. When the floods come against my soul, would You help me remember that? Would you draw my attention to Your heart so I can worship You?*

## YOU ARE MY FAVORITE

*T*HERE'S NO ONE more important to Me than you. There's no one I'd rather spend time with more than you. There's no one I love more than you. There's no one quite like you. I want you to get this—really get this. You are unique. You are special. You are My favorite. I love you completely and just as you are. Nothing will ever change that—nothing. You can rest in that reality.

EPHESIANS 2:10; PSALM 139; 1 JOHN 4:10

### ✣ PRAYER ✣

*I feel the same way about You. You are awesome and mighty. You are beautiful and faithful. There is no one else like You. Thank You for Your commitment to me. Thank You for sharing Your heart with me. Thank You for always standing by my side.*

## December 22

### YOU ARE SECURE

*P*EOPLE MAY BE fickle at times. You never know what to expect from some people. You never know if they are really with you and for you. But know this: I am not fickle. I do not change. I am not moody. I will not turn you away. I am always the same. You are secure in My love. You are secure.

1 John 5:13; Philippians 4:19; Psalm 4:8

### ✦ PRAYER ✦

*Your character is unshakable. Even when I am on an emotional roller coaster, You are steady. Thank You for being an anchor for my soul in turbulent times. Teach me how to embrace the security that belongs to me in Christ.*

## Let Go of Regrets

*R*EGRETS ARE NOT worth carrying. Regrets are a heavy burden that weighs you down. Regrets hinder your forward progress. Imagine how much faster you could run the race set before you—the race Father has given you to run—if you were to let go of the regrets. The enemy will always remind you of what you didn't do or what you should have done. I'm reminding you not to listen.

2 THESSALONIANS 3:16; JAMES 3:18;
HEBREWS 12:1

### ✦ PRAYER ✦

*Father's Word tells me to lay aside the weights*
*that slow me down. Would You show me any*
*hidden regret in my heart? Would You teach me*
*how to discern bitterness in my speech? Would*
*You free me from the residue of resentment?*
*I declare that I will not live in regret.*

## December 24

## I Am Listening for Your Prayers

Sometimes you forget to lean on Me. I stand by with a heart full of comfort and counsel, with abundant grace available, and with all the wisdom you need to move for Me. It grieves Me to watch you struggle along on some days, walking in your own strength, when I am waiting and watching for you to look My way. I am listening for your prayer of help. Lean on Me and not on your own understanding.

1 John 5:14; 1 Peter 3:12; Psalm 55:17

### ✦ Prayer ✦

*I don't want to grieve You in any way, ever.
But I have learned to be self-sufficient through
the circumstances of my life. Show me how
to let go and let You do what You do best.
Teach me not to depend on myself in areas
where I should be depending on You.*

## I WANT TO SHOW YOU THE POWER OF THE BLOOD

*Y*OU'VE ONLY SKIMMED the surface of the revelation of the blood of Jesus. You've heard that the blood cleanses you from all unrighteousness, that there is atonement in the blood. You've heard that you were redeemed by the shed blood of Christ unto salvation, which includes healing and deliverance. But there is so much more I want you to see about the power of the blood. Study to show yourself approved.

1 JOHN 1:7; HEBREWS 9:14; REVELATION 12:11

### → PRAYER ←

*I sing songs about the blood of Jesus and recite Scriptures about the power in the blood, but I know that I see and know only in part. Teach me all I need to know about what the blood of Christ accomplished. Show me what that practically means to my life, and I will show others.*

## December 26

### I AM YOUR ANCHOR

*I* AM YOUR ANCHOR. I will keep you steady in the midst of the raging storm. Because you have set your love upon Me, because you have set your heart toward Me, I will hold you up when the winds of adversity blow. Set your mind upon Me in the face of trouble, and I will present you with peace. I am your anchor. I have you.

HEBREWS 6:19; PSALM 91:14; JOEL 2:12

### → PRAYER ←

*You set my feet like hind's feet. You empower me to go through trouble and trials. Remind me of Your presence in the midst of the battle. Show me how to stand strong against the hurricane-force winds that are intent on knocking me down.*

## LOVE THEM ANYWAY

*N*OT EVERYONE WHO wants to be your friend has friendly motives. Love them anyway. Not everyone who comes into your life making big promises intends to keep them. Love them anyway. Jesus knew from the beginning that Judas would betray Him. But He loved Him anyway. Learn to love your enemies as you love your friends. Love guards your heart.

1 CORINTHIANS 13:4–8; LUKE 6:35;
LEVITICUS 19:18

### ✦ PRAYER ✦

*Let love motivate every word I speak and every action I take. Teach me how to love those who hate me. Show me how to bless those who are intent on taking from me. Help me learn how to guard my heart from the offenses that will come.*

## December 28

### Your Sacrificial Praise Pleases Me

Obedience is better than sacrifice, yet the sacrifice of praise is a beautiful thing to My ears. I take delight in your willingness and your obedience because it allows Father to fulfill His promise to let you eat the good of the land. Yet I know that lifting your voice in praise sometimes contradicts the desires of your soul. Your sacrificial praise pleases Me.

1 Samuel 15:22; Isaiah 1:19; Hebrews 13:15

### → Prayer ←

*Give me the grace of obedience. Give me a mouth that praises You and a heart that sings for joy in Your presence. Help me press past the flesh, which wars against Your Spirit. Teach me how to let my spirit lead the way and how to crucify my uncooperative flesh.*

## DISCERN YOUR TIMES AND SEASONS

O EVERYTHING THERE is a season. Discern the season you're in, and you will respond rightly to situations and circumstances. When you are in a season of sowing, sow—and know that a harvest season is coming. When you are in a season of pruning, don't resist. War and fight, but know that a season of new growth is coming. Discern your times and seasons.

PSALM 1:3; MATTHEW 24:32; JOHN 15

### ⚜ PRAYER ⚜

*The gift of discerning of spirits dwells on the inside of me, but I don't always discern shifts in season soon enough. Would You sharpen me in that area? Would You teach me how to recognize the shift before it happens so I can prepare my heart for what's ahead?*

## I Will Give You Courage
## to Move Forward

REGARDING THOSE WHO would walk away, let them go. Bless them as they go. Don't try to hold on to people who decide to depart. Instead, turn to Me. I am right beside you. I will give you the courage to move forward with new strength, even in the face of disappointing departures. Many times those disappointing departures are divine interventions. Not everyone who comes into your life is meant to be there.

JOHN 16:33; PSALM 16:8; ISAIAH 12:2

### ✦ PRAYER ✦

*I am learning. I am leaning on You. You know what is best for me and who is best for my life. You know who will walk with me and who will walk away before they ever come into my life. Help me to hear Your voice about every relationship before I enter into it. Show me Your will in the matter.*

## TAKE STOCK OF YOUR LIFE

WHAT ARE THE desires of your heart? What do you really want out of life? Before we enter the New Year, take some time to talk with Me and pray to Father in the name of Jesus. I will help you pray. Let Me give you the clarity you need to move forward in Father's will and to determine what you need to do differently to see the desires of your heart come to pass. Father won't do your part, but He will do His part. Will you do your part? Prepare your heart for the next season and determine to press in. You'll be glad you did.

PSALM 37:4; JEREMIAH 29:11; JAMES 1:17

### ⇒ PRAYER ⇐

*I will do my part—if I know what it is. Please show me how to prepare for the year ahead. Please teach me how to walk in the promises of God. Help me walk in Father's perfect will and delight myself in Him. Give me Your desires for my life, and I will pursue them.*

# CONNECT WITH US!

**CHARISMA HOUSE**

( Spiritual Growth )

Facebook.com/CharismaHouse

@CharismaHouse

Instagram.com/CharismaHouseBooks

## SILOAM

( Health )

Pinterest.com/CharismaHouse

## REALMS

( Fiction )

Facebook.com/RealmsFiction